The Political Collapse of Europe

THE
Political Collapse
OF
Europe

BY

Hajo Holborn
YALE UNIVERSITY

GREENWOOD PRESS, PUBLISHERS
WESTPORT, CONNECTICUT

Library of Congress Cataloging in Publication Data

Holborn, Hajo, 1902-1969.
    The political collapse of Europe.

    Reprint. Originally published: 1st ed. New York :
Knopf, 1951 (1965 printing)
    Bibliography: p.
    Includes index.
    1. Europe--Politics and government--20th century.
I. Title.
D424.H6 1982   940.2'8   82-11839
ISBN 0-313-23031-5 (lib. bdg.)

Reprinted with the permission of Alfred A. Knopf, Inc.

Reprinted in 1982 by Greenwood Press
A division of Congressional Information Service, Inc.
88 Post Road West, Westport, Connecticut 06881

Printed in the United States of America

10 9 8 7 6 5 4 3 2 1

Foreword

THIS book is an attempt at historical interpretation rather than a historical narrative of events. The narration has been confined to the minimum necessary for the understanding of the great sweep of historical events that transformed the face of Europe and the course of world history resting squarely on the shoulders of the old Continent in the nineteenth century. Inevitably, a historical review of this type must deal with some basic events rather sketchily, because they are well known, whereas some less-explored forces and developments must be discussed in greater detail if they seem to throw additional light on the historical origins of the situation in which we find ourselves today.

Historical research has a twofold purpose. Its most immediate task is to assemble the record of events. But the work of the historian necessarily must also aim at the understanding of these events. Without an interpretation of history, historical study remains a learned pursuit that has no direct bearing upon the intellectual and political decisions that the living generation must make. Such decisions do not simply follow from history. Every generation faces new problems and responds to them with its own peculiar strength and attitude. But the issues that confront mankind can be solved only if they are conceived of as part of a never ending historical process, to which all of us have to submit. The movement of history does not terminate at some point in the past designated by historians because they cannot find any printed sources beyond a given date. No doubt the character of our available sources determines the character of our historical knowledge and insight, but there can be no question that history must be interpreted as an evolution, of which our present age is a mere part. If so, we should make every effort to relate the history of the past to our present vital concerns and try in particular to recover the knowledge about the day before yesterday that has slipped from living memory and not been caught by the professional historian.

I am indebted to Mr. Robert H. Ferrell for his warm interest in the appearance of this book and his active assistance in the preparation of the bibliography. I gratefully record the permission of the editors of *World Politics* to draw freely on my article "The Collapse of the European Political System, 1914–45" published in the July, 1949, issue. Both my children, Frederick and Hanna, to whom this book is dedicated, made many useful suggestions. I am under deep obligation to my wife, Annemarie Holborn, for her untiring endeavor to improve the style and contents of the book and for assuming the heavy burden of all the technical work.

Hajo Holborn

New Haven, Conn.

Contents

Introduction

FOR many centuries, in fact for more than a millennium, Europe had a political order of her own and the strength to defend herself against invaders. She was many times hard pressed by foreign conquerors such as the Saracens, Tartars, or Turks, and over long periods various countries remained under the heel of non-European rulers. But in spite of her internal dissensions, which often enough had invited attacks from the outside, Europe emerged after the seventeenth century as the absolute master of her own political fortunes. Moreover, she sent thousands of settlers to the shores of the New World, who planted Western civilization overseas, and gained colonial dominion over foreign races in other regions of the world. As the Russian empire arose, it was limited on the West by Europe; nevertheless, all through the eighteenth and nineteenth centuries it seemed likely that Russia, though, like Britain, extending into far-off parts of the world, would become another great European state.

The independence of the American colonies and the creation of an American nation-state comprising the major part of the North American continent made far-sighted political observers like Alexis de Tocqueville predict that the dominant position of the European nations in world affairs would come to an end in a not too distant future. But nineteenth century developments seemed to belie the divination of the great historical thinker. Europe appeared to burst forth with ever new energy. She was the center of the expanding world economy as well as the heart and brain of Western civilization, which was thought to be destined to transform all the other civilizations after its own image. The vigorous peoples of this continent did not seem to have lost their capacity for settling their own political problems.

Admittedly, relations among the European nations were tense and peaceful methods of diplomacy precarious. Statesmen knew that recourse to war had become a growing threat to the very foundations of Europe, but they did not anticipate that, if the worst happened, Europe could not retrieve a European political order by her own military and political efforts. But their security proved unfounded. The general war among the European nations that broke out in August, 1914, did not bring clear military and political decisions. World War I was finally decided by American intervention. For a moment it seemed that the old European political system was going to be replaced by a world-wide system. Actually, no world-wide security system came into existence after 1919; yet only the façades of a European system remained standing. In World War II, which was decided by the participation of the Soviet Union and the United States, the collapse of the traditional European system became an irrevocable fact. What is commonly called the "historic Europe" is dead and beyond resurrection.

It is doubtful to what extent this statement has become common knowledge. There exists, of course, a general awareness of radical changes in world politics and especially in European affairs. But in the formulation of American policies serious mistakes have been committed owing to the belief that a return to a Europe fundamentally similar to that of the nineteenth century could be effected. We still are consciously or unconsciously influenced by what we consider to be the "normal" structure and are thereby led to direct our political actions as much as possible toward the restoration of the traditional order.

On the other hand, America's practical experiences in European politics demonstrate that American policy makers are constantly driven to adopt unprecedented measures that run counter to the historical concept of a European pattern. From this unforeseen novelty of the present European situation it has also been inferred that we could forget its history altogether. But such an inference could lead to even more serious blunders. It could lead the United States to frame its policy under the spur of the moment and exclusively from the point of view of a narrowly defined national expediency. Yet, though the self-contained European political system has broken down and Europe finds herself under the shadow of two world rivals, her nations are not dead. And they were moulded by the old European system, under which they developed their national characteristics as well as a common European consciousness.

The collapse of the traditional political system of Europe took place at the same time that the self-contained American political system of the nineteenth century disappeared. For more than thirty-five years the United States has made herself a partner to all the great political decisions of Europe. The history of the political collapse of Europe contains, therefore, a long sequence of American participation and has to be reappraised in the light of our present situation.

A constructive treatment of Europe's present-day problems calls for historical thinking, which is something more than mere historical knowledge. The foremost task of historical interpretation is the establishment of a clear distinction between the forces and ideas of former ages that continue to be alive and those that have ceased to be issues in our time or, perhaps, forever. Only such historical evaluation and perspective can enable us to act with discerning judgment.

The Political Collapse of Europe

TO MY CHILDREN

Hanna and Frederick

I

THE HISTORIC EUROPE AND THE

RISE OF RUSSIA

FOR almost a thousand years Europe meant the community of Western peoples who lived, broadly speaking, between Scandinavia and Sicily, the British Isles and the Pripet marshes. This statement is a great over-simplification of a very complex historical and geographical situation. For eight centuries most of the Iberian peninsula was under Saracen control, and for a long period the Balkans and the lower Danube basin were dominated by the Turks. Magyar, Slav, and Mongol invasions moved the eastern frontiers of Europe back and forth through the ages.

In view of the fluctuations of her southern, southeastern, and eastern boundaries Europe cannot be defined clearly by strict geographical principles. In geographical terms one could describe it only as the western peninsula of the Eurasian Continent, surrounded by the Atlantic Ocean and its two eastward extensions, the Mediterranean and Baltic Seas. These seas distinguish Europe sharply from the unbroken landmass of the East and form the most important single geographical precondition for the growth of a distinct western civilization.

Leopold Ranke, in his first work, defined Europe as the community of the Latin and Germanic nations.* But Eu-

* *Geschichte der romanischen und germanischen Völker von 1494 bis 1514,* first published in 1824. The third edition formed Vols. 33–4 of

rope was more than the western half of the Roman empire augmented by the Germanic world. Slav nations like
the Poles and Czechs formed an integral element in the
medieval and modern history of Europe. Once the Magyar
horsemen had settled down in the plains of the Danube
valley, they became stalwart defenders of Western civilization as did the Baltic peoples and the Finns. Moreover,
with the decline of the Turkish empire, the Yugoslav, Rumanian, Bulgarian, and Greek peoples joined Europe.

Europe never was a single political unit. Not even the
medieval emperors aspired to the creation of a universal
European state. They aimed at the establishment of a pre-
eminent position among the national kings, and even this
they rarely attained. The real ties of the European nations were cultural bonds. It is very often assumed that
the medieval Church would have liked to extinguish all
national differentiations. Yet on the contrary, the Roman
Church felt itself the guide and moulder of nations.
Against the universal claims of the emperors, the popes
called up the help of the national kings. The medieval
Church not only tolerated, but actually promoted, national
diversity. The Church demanded, it is true, the general
acceptance of its religious, moral, and intellectual teachings and attempted successfully to implant in the Western
nations a sense of common responsibility for the realization of a Christian order. The medieval society was by no
means a free society. Nevertheless, it was a civilization in
which no single principle dominated. Church and state retained a mutual independence in spite of the constant interaction between the ecclesiastical and political authorities.
Universalism and local diversification constituted another

L. Ranke: *Sämmtliche Werke* (Leipzig: 1885). For further elaboration
on Ranke's view of Europe cf. F. Meinecke: *"Germanischer und ro-
manischer Geist im Wandel der deutschen Geschichtsauffassung,"*
Historische Zeitschrift, (1917) Vol. CXV, and also in the same
author's collection *Preussen und Deutschland im 19. und 20. Jahrhundert* (Munich: 1918), pp. 100–24. Compare also T. H. Von Laue:
Leopold Ranke, The Formative Years (Princeton: 1950), pp. 24 ff.

pair of fruitful opposites. The dynamic character of Western history must be explained largely by the coexistence of such counterbalancing forces and ideas. No doubt they made for conflict, but they also raised human energies to high levels.

The Western Church passed on to Europe a great deal of the Greco-Roman cultural heritage. The study of Greek was discontinued for centuries, but the Church carried on much of the rational spirit of classic Greece. The Western Church did not consider the Christian faith a matter of mere sentiment or of blind adherence to traditional rituals. The philosophical and logical treatment of religion—in other words, theology—was a primary interest of the medieval Church and under its roof Greek philosophical thought continued to influence Western thinking, just as Roman law lived on in the outward church organization. After the tenth century classical knowledge steadily expanded. With the rise of a more highly differentiated society and the disappearance of the clergy's monopoly on education, the classical world began to be studied as the model of a mundane society. The stage was prepared for the age of the Renaissance.

Protestantism loosened the synthesis of ideas and institutions on which medieval Europe had rested. Christian universalism suffered from the ensuing ecclesiastical split. On the whole the Protestant churches tended to strengthen local forces and in many cases readily compromised with the existing political authorities, although at the same time Protestantism emphasized the relative independence of the individual in spiritual matters. But Protestantism did not revolutionize the basic pattern of European civilization. Like the Roman Catholic faith Protestantism was an active and reasoned creed capable of, and in need of, philosophical argument. The ancient heritage was well preserved in Protestantism.

The collapse of religious unity and the catastrophe of the wars of religion dethroned theology as the regulating force of Western culture. Philosophy and science took its place. The eighteenth century enlightenment expressed many of the deep longings that Christianity had raised in the hearts of the Western peoples, but it departed radically from the former transcendental interpretation of life. The enlightenment placed its faith in human reason. In the eyes of the modern philosophers, human reason had demonstrated its creative capacity by the production of modern science, which went infinitely beyond what the Greeks had ever achieved. But modern Western science not only enormously enhanced man's control of nature; it also seemed to grant him the power of organizing social and human conditions. The American and French revolutions translated these philosophical ideas into programs of political action.

The disappointments brought about by the course of the French Revolution and the wars that followed in its wake modified the original optimism that had anticipated an easy transformation of human affairs toward a final and ideal stage. The importance of historical traditions was discovered, and there was an ever growing awareness of the nonrational forces of life. Still, though liberals and conservatives disagreed sharply on the extent to which man was master of the world's destiny, nineteenth century thought as a whole held that history had an irresistible forward momentum and that the human race was bound to advance.

At least there was no doubt in the minds of Western men that the West would overpower and permeate all the other civilizations. In 1879, one year after the Congress of Berlin, which had nearly eliminated Turkish power over European soil and nations, the eighty-four year old Leopold Ranke re-edited a book on the history of Serbia that he had written half a century before. The father of modern historical research, a devout Christian conservative, added an epilogue in which he attempted to define Western civilization and to explain the reasons for its expansion.

The Ottoman Empire [he wrote] has been mastered
and penetrated in all directions by the spirit of Christianity. If we talk of the "spirit of Christianity" we
do not only have in mind religion. The words "culture" and "civilization" also would express it very in-
completely. It is the genius of the Occident. It is the
spirit that transforms peoples into organized armies,
builds roads, digs canals, covers the oceans with navies
and transforms them into possessions and fills the distant continents with colonies. It explores the depths of
nature through exact research, takes possession of all
fields of knowledge, and continually renews them by
fresh efforts without losing sight of the eternal truth
which administers order and law among men in spite
of the variety of their passions. We see this spirit in
a state of extraordinary progress. It has won America
from the rough forces of nature and intractable peoples. It pushes into the most remote Asia. China is
hardly closed any longer and Africa is surrounded on
all her shores. Irresistibly, in many guises, unassail-
ably, armed with weapons and science, the spirit of the
Occident subdues the world. . . .*

There is no direct reference in Ranke's remarks to Russia, which did more than any other power to free the
Balkan nations from Turkish rule during the nineteenth
century. Apparently Ranke was convinced that Russia had
become so westernized as to be considered a full member
of the community of Western nations.

But the whole problem of the westernization of the
world should be reappraised in the light of our modern
historical experiences. The modern Americas were not
"westernized"; they were Western from the beginning.
American history rested on the migration of European civilization in the course of which the small native population was dispossessed, as in North America, by a rapidly

* Serbien und die Türkei im neunzehnten Jahrhundert, in Sämmtliche Werke (Leipzig: 1879), Vols. 43–4, pp. 518–19 [my translation].

growing population of European immigrants or, as in Latin America, was subjugated and remoulded by much smaller bands of conquering Europeans. The civilization of the Americas is merely the extension of Western civilization to the New World. New national forms of high vitality and great potentiality were added to the older national types of Europe. But the Atlantic Ocean, across which the new inhabitants were carried to the western shores, never proved a major cultural divide between America and Europe. Even today an average American citizen is closer to the average Englishman or Scandinavian than any of the three would be to a Spaniard. On the other hand, a Latin American usually feels closer to Spanish, French, or Italian culture than to that of the United States.

Only where Western civilization met one of the old historic civilizations like the Russian, Turkish, East Indian, or Chinese can we sensibly talk of "westernization." This term refers not to the replacement of the other civilizations, but to only a certain degree of adaptation to Western ideas and institutions. The modern secularized West has shown itself to be the power to which the other living civilizations easily succumbed. All of them, in various degrees, have accepted Western scientific and technological methods and are well on their way to using them successfully. Together with the adoption of science went the Western belief in historical progress and the capacity of human reason to produce social betterment. But the human and moral values that in the history of Western civilization have directed the use of man's power over nature and society have not been fully transmitted.

Westernization of the world is the single dominant fact of modern history, but it has created new divisions as well as new bonds. Some of these divisions stem from Western civilization itself, since it has been not only diversified nationally and religiously but also divided socially and ideologically. These Western conflicts have been carried over into the world at large. The international civil war in which our present generation lives is to a large extent the result of internal Western tensions. But other factors and causes must be considered as well.

In all these events the civilization most closely related to the West by geographical proximity, cultural contacts, and, during the last 250 years, by political association, has played a decisive role. There is no good historical reason why Russia or sections of Russia should be considered a part of the Western world. Herodotus called the Caucasus mountains and the Don river the boundaries of the civilized world. When the humanist Von Herberstein went to Moscow on a diplomatic mission for the Emperor Maximilian in the early years of the sixteenth century, he felt that he was venturing into Asia.* Maps of that period showed the Ural mountains as "the belt of the earth" beyond which China began.

In the eighteenth and nineteenth centuries the Russian Government chose to call the Ural mountains and river the line of division between a European and Asiatic Russia. But this stipulated line is only of historical interest. It reflected the strong westward orientation of Russian policy inaugurated by Peter the Great and, negatively, Russia's physical inability to integrate the endless continental expanse beyond the Urals into the Russian empire. But just as the United States turned the American West into an integral part of the Republic largely in the half-century before 1890, so Russia succeeded in amalgamating its "Asiatic" territories during the half-century thereafter. Czarist Russia began this development with the building of the trans-Siberian railroad, and the Soviets continued it with the construction of their central Asia railroad network, completing it with their seemingly anti-colonial and federal policies. The Urals are not a dividing line in modern Russia. As a matter of fact, the adjacent territories east and west of this relatively insignificant mountain range and river belong today to the R.S.F.S.R., the Russian Soviet Republic. Now trains shuttle back and forth from

* S. von Herberstein: *Rerum Moscoviticarum commentarii* (Vienna: 1549).

the west, south, and east to maintain this region. It was
significant that Kubishev, to the south of the Urals, was
made the capital of the Soviet Union when the Germans
threatened Moscow in 1941, as it was symbolic, too, that
four years later Mongolian divisions were among the Russian troops that fought their way into Berlin.

Russia has been a Eurasian country from her beginnings.
In contrast to Europe her contacts with the classical world
were slight. The Greek trading posts on the southern coast
of the Black Sea were destroyed in the second Christian
century by central Asiatic tribes like the Sarmates or Huns
who used the route along the shores of the Black Sea.
Nowhere in Russia was there a continuity of settlement
from classical days such as we find not only in Italy and
France but also in Britain and even important sections of
Germany. The conversion of the eastern Slavs occurred relatively late in history and after a lengthy period of separation from the Mediterranean world. The early Russian
state of Kiev accepted Christianity from Byzantium in the
tenth century.

The relations between Byzantium and Russia are mostly
exaggerated. Byzantium was too proud to care much about
the organization of her foreign ecclesiastical dependencies.
In the thirteenth century Russia was cut off from Byzantium by the Tartar invasion, and by the time she emerged
from Tartar domination Byzantium had fallen to the
Turks. Rome's influence on the Latin and even on the Germanic and western Slav nations was more intimate and
was sustained over a longer period of time than that of
Byzantium over the eastern Slavs. The Russian Church,
particularly prior to the late fifteenth century, was not a
mere replica of the Church of Byzantium. The Tartar invasion practically destroyed the whole indigenous political
organization of Russia, and it seemed for a while that the
Russian Church would acquire a position similar to the
Western rather than to the Byzantine Church. But the
grand dukes of Moscow proved in the end the liberators
from the Tartar yoke, and this fact enabled the Czars after

1480 to subordinate the Russian Church to the state in Byzantine fashion.

From the late fifteenth century onward the Russian Church displayed the characteristic traits of Byzantine organization and piety. Whereas the Roman Church preserved a great deal of the rational and philosophical achievements of Greece together with the Roman determination to change the existing world, Byzantium had chiefly preserved the Greek aesthetic vision. Symbols and the dramatic ritual counted more in the Eastern Church than theology. The deep enthusiasm aroused by the adumbration of the beauty of the transcendental world left relatively little room for co-ordinated social action. The Eastern Church has, indeed, taught the Christian virtues of brotherly love, forgiveness, charity, and humility to its faithful. The Western conscience was strongly moved by the glow of this piety as shown in the works of such writers as Dostojevski and Tolstoy. But the Russian Church never demanded a Christian reform of worldly conditions. It left the management of the secular order to the state, which was at the same time the protector of the orthodox faith and ritual of the Church.

Not even through its church did the Russian civilization inherit much Greek and Roman thought. This fact by itself could explain why there were no renascences of antiquity in Russian history. But it should not be forgotten that, in the age of the Western European Renaissance, Russia had still not recovered from the cruel devastations suffered by her urban centers during the Tartar invasion. It is quite conceivable that without the Tartar invasions Russia would have moved closer culturally to the West. As it was, the Renaissance forms that some Italian architects used in the erection of the great Kremlin wall and other Kremlin buildings were of no consequence to the future development of Russian culture. During the three centuries before 1700 the contrast between Russian and Western civilization hardened, and this contrast has not been overcome by the westernization of Russia in the subsequent two-and-

1-half centuries. During all stages the Russian Government was able to use Western ideas and institutions merely as means for the strengthening of its absolute power.

In all other countries, with the possible exception of Japan, westernization occurred as the result of outright colonial conquest or, as in the case of Turkey, of military defeat, or of strong Western economic control; but Russia used westernization from the outset as a means for her own expansion and conquest. Although culturally divided from Europe, she soon became one of the great powers in the European political system. The rise of Russia to this position took place in less than a century. As one might expect, westernization, begun under Peter the Great, first appeared in military affairs. Peter took over from the Dutch and Swedes the best that the military science and professional tactics of the age could offer. With his new army he defeated Charles XII of Sweden at Poltava in 1709. His victory gave Russia most of the Swedish possessions on the northeastern shores of the Baltic. This success also deprived Sweden and her French ally of their preponderant influence in Poland. In 1735 a Russian army installed the Russian favorite, August III of Saxony, as king of Poland, and shortly thereafter this army proceeded to the Rhine to join forces with the German imperial army under Prince Eugene, who conducted his last campaign against the French.

In the Seven Years' War the Russian army fought two major battles against Frederick the Great. The first was one of the costliest victories in the king's military career; the second one, the battle of Kunersdorf, a defeat that almost ended it. In the next year, 1760, the Russians for the first time reached the Prussian capital as conquerors. It was, incidentally, from Kunersdorf that Marshal Zhukov launched his final offensive against Berlin in April 1945. In 1770 a Russian fleet sailed through the Straits of Gibraltar to gain the victory of Tschesme over Turkish naval forces. Twenty years later Russian troops landed in Holland and a Russian army under Suvorov fought in northern Italy.

It is interesting to note that Suvorov has been built up in the Russia of Stalin as one of the great heroes of Russian history. Between 1709 and 1799 Russia had acquired the Baltic provinces and a major part of Poland, had reached the Black Sea, and had gained for her merchant vessels access to the Mediterranean through the Turkish Straits. Her military and political influence was felt all over Europe.

II

THE POLITICAL FOUNDATIONS

OF MODERN EUROPE

1. THE EUROPEAN BALANCE OF POWER

EUROPE never formed a self-contained po-
litical unit. At all times neighboring civilizations influenced
her political fortunes and were even able to make great in-
roads into the Continent. The Arab and Byzantine civilizations in the Middle Ages, the Turkish and Russian empires
in the modern age exercised tremendous pressures upon Europe that were amplified by the national dissensions of the
Continent. The greatest single example was the Franco-
Turkish alliance of 1536 concluded by the "most Christian" King of France against "the apostolic majesty"
Charles V, who with his combined rule over Austria,
Spain, the Netherlands, Italy, and parts of the German empire seemed about to turn the French kingdom into a province of his universal monarchy.

In the Middle Ages the feeling of Christian unity
against foreign adversaries was not so strong as the Cru-
sades might indicate, and it had become feeble with the
rise of the national states at the end of the Middle Ages
and in the early modern period.* The feeling of a com-

* W. Fritzemeyer: *Christenheit und Europa* (Leipzig: 1931);
F. L. Baumer: "England, the Turk, and the Common Corps of Chris-
tendom," *American Historical Review* (1945), Vol. L, pp. 26–48.

mon Christian responsibility did not disappear altogether, but it was assumed that this responsibility consisted chiefly of maintaining the independence of the existing Christian nations and their capacity to make their existence secure against the threat of a universal monarchy. Cardinal Wolsey is generally credited with having launched a deliberate policy of creating a European balance. He was the first English statesman to attempt to equalize the changing weights of the Bourbon and Habsburg monarchies by shifting English support from one side to the other. At the same time France even carried the idea of balance beyond the Christian community; from the days of Francis I to Louis XV, France used her alliance with Turkey to weaken the power of the Habsburgs. The France of Henry IV and Richelieu exploited also the division between Catholics and Protestants. The Peace of Westphalia of 1648 was founded on both a political and a religious balance. Similarly England, after she had weathered the Spanish danger and was faced with Louis XIV's bid for hegemony, attempted to mobilize Protestant support under Cromwell and even more so under William III. The axis built around England, the Netherlands, and Austria became in the days of Marlborough and Prince Eugene the political instrument for bringing French expansion to a standstill.

England in the eighteenth century also welcomed within certain limits the rise of Russia.* Russia's defeat of Sweden seemed to establish an equilibrium of power in the Baltic that would guarantee English access to this region, the source of stores on which the English navy depended. Russia's progress against the other ally of France, Turkey, was similarly applauded by England, since it strengthened the British naval position in the Mediterranean, then based on Gibraltar and the Balearic Islands. The Russian fleet was led to victory at Tschesme by British officers in Russian service.

---

* Cf. the excellent study by D. Gerhard: *England und der Aufstieg Russlands* (Munich: 1933).

The sense of loyalty to a common Christian cause had thus largely vanished at the beginnings of modern history. At least the courts and chancelleries were little affected by whatever popular sentiment of this sort continued to exist. Furthermore, the inter-European groupings of states were grounded on clear religious principles no more than their relations to non-Western powers were ruled by their common religious or cultural traditions.

Yet the balance-of-power policy of the eighteenth century did not submerge the feeling of Western unity altogether. After all, the Turks had lost their terror in recent centuries, and it could be hoped that the Russians, under their enlightened if somewhat strange rulers, would adapt themselves to the West. The balance-of-power theory meanwhile afforded a general rule of the game. It made politics more calculable. Since the rule was invented to make it impossible for a single power to make overwhelming gains, it also enabled the individual state to avoid unnecessary losses. Moreover, since the operation of the balance-of-power system presupposed the existence of a number of larger states, it appeared most unlikely that any major European nation would perish under it. When the Polish partitions of 1772, 1793, and 1795 demonstrated that even a large country could be destroyed, the Western world was profoundly shocked. Jefferson always considered the destruction of Poland a historic event as significant as the French Revolution.

One of the reasons for the disturbance of the traditional order of Europe in the latter half of the eighteenth century was the preoccupation of the Western powers with their struggle for colonial domination. Particularly in English eyes the battlegrounds in Europe were of minor significance compared with those in the West Indies or in the American colonies. Such an attitude was hardly favorable to a circumspect European policy. The growth of Russian power was favored by this English attitude. French policy was deeply divided by the counsels of the continental and colonial schools. The Franco-Turkish alliance, for example,

1: *The European Balance of Power*

lost its practical meaning when France in 1756 concluded
an alliance with the archenemies of Turkey—Russia and
Austria. In central Europe the conflict between her neighbors and Prussia made easy Russia's advance into the
West.

The elder Pitt knew that active participation in continental affairs was a vital necessity for Britain, even if she
wanted for herself only colonial and naval supremacy. But
the wisdom of this political maxim was hidden to many
Englishmen, who judged that England either should avoid
all continental entanglements or should drop her continental allies once she had gained her own aims. The most no-
torious example of this policy was the British desertion of
the alliance with Prussia in the Seven Years' War, which
placed Frederick the Great in mortal danger and made
him an implacable foe of Britain. When the American colonies declared their independence, Britain had no friends
on the Continent, but found both France and Spain, and
also in a small way Prussia, ready to support the revolutionary colonists. Pitt said that England had conquered
America in Germany during the Seven Years' War. It
could also be said that she lost America not only at
Yorktown but also in Europe.

During the Revolutionary and Napoleonic wars, Britain,
by her bold, steadfast, and high-principled conduct, succeeded in defeating Napoleon's attempt at the creation of a
universal European monarchy and in laying the foundation
of a new British empire to take the place of the first
British empire that had been wrecked by the American
war. Except for the brief interval of a year in 1802–03
Britain was at war with France from 1792 to 1815. She
fought France with varying European coalitions and, for a
number of years, all by herself. It was her good luck that
by the time she stood alone, her naval supremacy had been
safely established by Nelson's heroic victories. Napoleon
could not hope to invade the British Isles and had to fall
back on economic warfare. The closing of all of the Continent to English commodities and products was expected

to upset the British balance of payments and force Britain to accept peace on French conditions.

But this mercantilistic scheme, known as the Continental System, did not achieve its objectives. The British, though they had lost the American colonies, had not lost their American commerce and were able to expand it. British financial credit also proved much greater than contemporaries had believed. On the French side the enforcement of the scheme was inadequate. The administrative controls needed for the full realization of the plan had not yet been developed. Nor did the French Government itself possess a blind determination to adhere to the system. The blockade was a double-edged sword that threatened the enemy but also wounded the bearer. The attempted elimination of English trade from the Continent created serious economic dislocations. Maybe Napoleon did not have to feel concern about the hardships that the defeated nations suffered, but it was disquieting to a French ruler to observe that the damage done to French trade was only partly made up by the prosperity of certain French industries. England, economically advanced and commercially strong, retained a powerful economic hold on the Continent, especially in countries of undeveloped and agrarian economy.

With the defeat of Austria in 1805 and of Prussia in the following year, Europe to the Vistula was in Napoleon's grip, and he began to organize it according to his will. Between 1805 and 1807 Napoleon also beat the Russian armies that had supported Austria and Prussia. In the Peace of Tilsit, Czar Alexander I and Napoleon concluded an uneasy compromise. Napoleon did not wipe Prussia off the map completely, though the remaining rump-Prussia could not very well be considered a buffer between France and Russia. In deference to Alexander's susceptibilities Poland was not fully restored. Nevertheless, Napoleon was not satisfied with the Russian recognition of his continental conquest, but wanted active Russian co-operation in the war against Britain. Yet to adhere more than superficially to the Continental System would have been ruinous for the

Russian economy. The Czar believed, furthermore, that active Russian support of France against Britain required greater French assistance for Russian plans in Turkey and a guarantee against the resurrection of the Kingdom of Poland. For where would Alexander stand when Napoleon had really crushed Britain?

Thus Napoleon and Alexander soon drifted apart, and the French Emperor then decided to subdue the last major power that opposed his authority on the Continent. The catastrophe that befell the *grande armée*—the greatest army ever assembled by an empire in world history up to that time—in the wide spaces and the fierce winter of Russia suddenly changed the whole world situation. The first move was now up to the Czar. Was the Russian army to carry the war into central and western Europe and to turn the patriotic Russian resistance into a war of European liberation from Napoleon? The old-Russian party, represented chiefly by Kutusov, commander of the army, warned the Czar against participation in a general European war. The Russian army could instead have stopped at the frontiers of Poland and could possibly still have occupied East Prussia. This move would have given Russia, which had acquired Finland a few years before, a dominant position in the Baltic, and with her northern flank protected, she could have turned her full attention to the Balkans and the Black Sea. From a Russian point of view it would then have been irrelevant who ruled central and western Europe.

The Soviet historian Eugene Tarlé, in his notable book on Napoleon's invasion of Russia in 1812* written in the heyday of Soviet isolationism, argued that Kutusov was right and that Alexander I spent Russian blood and strength gratuitously in entering the European arena. The outcome of such a war could only have been the establishment of a British-dominated Europe, in which Russia with her far inferior economy was bound to suffer. Undoubtedly Britain turned out to be the chief winner in 1815, but

* E. Tarlé: *Napoleon's Invasion of Russia, 1812* (New York: 1942) (first Russian edition, Moscow: 1938).

Russia's gains achieved in the course of the wars of 1813–15 were, as we shall see, by no means negligible.

Alexander I combined in his weak nature the politico-religious traditions of Russia and the ideas of the French enlightenment, which his tutor LaHarpe had infused in him. His decision to continue the war against Napoleon was apparently made shortly after the fire of Moscow, largely under the influence of Baron Stein, who thereby gained an even higher stature in history than he had gained as the leading reform minister of Prussia in the year after the Peace of Tilsit. Stein's aim was the complete expulsion of the French from central Europe and the rebuilding of a Germany more fully united than the Holy Empire as the rock that would dispel any future attempt to establish a single tyrannical authority over Europe. Stein believed that the proclamation of national war aims would set free the additional fighting spirit needed for the final defeat of Napoleon.

Alexander hoped that by becoming the liberator of the European nations he would gain the position of a general protector of the reorganized Europe, particularly if he favored the liberal forces. He did not forget, however, that the Russian interests had to be advanced realistically. He wanted to restore the Kingdom of Poland, but as a Russian dependency, and in 1814 he intended to install his accommodating ally King Bernadotte of Sweden, a former French marshal, as king of France, a move that would have turned France, the second largest continental power, into a western outpost of Russia.

But the Russian and Swedish armies by themselves could not hope to defeat Napoleon in central Europe, and in the early spring of 1813, Prussia joined the struggle. Yet even though Prussia's enthusiastic war effort was prodigious compared with what could normally have been expected from a state of her size, the early military encounters between the anti-French coalition and Napoleon showed that Napoleon had sufficient strength at least to hold his own.

Austria now had her chance to become a major power

again. In 1809 Austria had appealed to German nationalism and had risen against Napoleon; but the war was a
costly failure. Austria was even more humiliated than she
had been four years earlier after Austerlitz. Since 1809,
when Metternich took over the direction of Austrian foreign policy, Austria had lived in practical submission to the
Napoleonic empire. The marriage of the Austrian Emper-
or's daughter Marie Louise to the French dictator was the
outward symbol of this new attitude. Metternich had believed in the success of Napoleon's invasion of Russia.
When confronted with its failure, however, he was not the
man to rush to Alexander's side. He sensed, of course, the
opportunities offered for the revival of an independent
Austrian policy, but such independence, he believed, could
be made lasting only through the restitution of the old
European balance of power. In his opinion nothing was to
be gained by replacing the "colossus of the West" by the
"colossus of the East." From his point of view it would
have been disastrous to let Russia gain a permanent foot-
hold in central Europe, not to mention western Europe.
Metternich therefore never favored the elimination of
France as one of the great powers of Europe. He went
further than that; he did not even think it desirable to
create in the center of Europe a highly unified Germany.
A strong Austria and a restored Prussia seemed to suffice
to protect central Europe against East and West.

There was a great deal of traditionalist sentiment and
prejudice in Metternich's opinions on German affairs, and
there was also fear of what the national idea might do to
the multinational Habsburg empire. But at the same time
he had a genuine concern in establishing a true European
equilibrium. When Metternich, who was born a Rhenish
count and whose ancestors had repeatedly occupied the
throne of the prince-archbishops of Trier, proposed in 1813
that France should evacuate Germany but keep the whole
left bank of the Rhine conquered by the French in the
early phase of the revolutionary wars, he showed that the
restoration of the balance of power in Europe was to him

of greater consequence than the sentimental attachment to the pre-revolutionary past. He was not even primarily interested in the removal of Napoleon; on the contrary, his offer to leave him the left bank of the Rhine was intended to make it possible for Napoleon to maintain himself on the French throne.

When Napoleon turned down Metternich's proposition, Austria went to war on the side of Russia and Prussia. But just after the allied armies had driven Napoleon over the Rhine and again before the allied armies occupied Paris, the Austrian chancellor persisted in presenting diplomatic schemes aimed at the preservation of a strong France under a ruler not amenable to foreign influence; and each time he halted or slowed up the military co-operation with the allied armies. Warfare was to him only the instrument of foreign policy, and it would have seemed a grave mistake if Austrian military strategy had overshot the mark at which Austrian diplomacy was aiming, namely, the re-establishment of the European balance of power. His wartime policy carefully laid the ground for the diplomacy that he followed at the Congress of Vienna. He would have preferred a compromise with Napoleon had the latter not been obstinate, but the return of Louis XVIII served his basic purpose, the exclusion from the French throne of any ruler under a special obligation to one of the other four great powers of Europe.

Metternich's policy of restoring the European balance of power would not have been successful if it had not been in harmony with the aims of the British Government. Not that Castlereagh and Metternich agreed on all issues. Castlereagh disliked the idea of leaving the lower and central Rhine valley in French hands. He wanted a rather strong Netherlands and to the east a military power capable of dealing with the threat of a new French invasion. Castlereagh achieved his objectives. France retained access only to the upper Rhine through Alsace. But the frontiers of 1792, restored in 1814, and even their trimmed version, the frontiers of 1790, imposed after Napoleon's return from Elba and his final defeat at Waterloo, left France more than she had owned before the revolution. Metternich's desire to avoid a humiliation of France was shared by Castlereagh.

Britain was in complete accord with Austria in the determination to limit Russian expansion to the west. This agreement was somewhat surprising. English policy in the first ten years of the revolutionary wars had been to draw Russia deeply into all parts of Europe including the Mediterranean in order to meet the French challenge. But the British were annoyed when they learned that the new Russian empire was pushing its protectionist economic policy with unrelenting vigor. In the early years of the new century Anglo-Russian trade relations were twice ruptured, since no mutually satisfactory trade treaty could be negotiated. British resentment was caused also by Russia's growing control of the whole Baltic Sea. The attacks of the British navy on Denmark were drastic, or, like the bombardment of Copenhagen in 1807, desperate, attempts at keeping the entrances of the Baltic open.

Anglo-Russian friction in the Baltic was supplemented by British fear of Russian influence in the Mediterranean, which had assumed a new political appearance; for Napoleon's expedition to Egypt in 1798-9 had opened up new vistas. The first British empire had been an Atlantic empire. India, which could be reached only by the long voyage around the South African cape, was a distant colony. In the second half of the eighteenth century the British India Company had extended its territories considerably, and the British had begun to penetrate into the Red Sea. But it was Napoleon's eagle eye that had perceived the future potentialities of the situation. He had recognized that Egypt and Suez, the eastern Mediterranean and the Red Sea were of major strategic significance for the new British empire, which had lost the American colonies. And, indeed, during the Napoleonic period India had gained in importance. Britain had not only excluded the French and Portuguese from that area but also had come to recognize the possibilities in the Suez route to India.*

The question in both French and British minds now became: Who was to rule the Middle Eastern countries? The Turkish empire and Persia did not seem capable of placing unsurmountable obstacles in the way of the Western powers, but if Russia were allowed to gain entrance into the eastern Mediterranean or control over Turkey, the Western powers would find stern resistance. British experience with the Russians in the Baltic and her concern with the future of the Middle East induced Castlereagh to oppose any extravagant expansion of Russian influence. Russia's place among the five major powers of Europe could not, of course, be contested, but she was not to be left in a position to threaten the balance of power.

At the Congress of Vienna, the so-called Polish-Saxon problem became the ultimate test of the new British policy. The resurrection of the Kingdom of Poland under Russian auspices was the foremost war aim of Alexander I. Prussia, saved from extinction by Russia in 1807 and empowered by the Russian victory of 1812 to fight for her liberation from France, could not demand from Russia the return of all her former Polish territories, which had extended to the central Vistula and had included Warsaw after the Third Partition of Poland in 1795. The Prussian Government therefore wanted as compensation the annexation of Saxony, her traditional competitor in northern Germany, who had fought to the end on Napoleon's side. The common front that Russia and Prussia presented at the Congress almost led to its breakdown and a war between the two powers and Britain, Austria, and France. But a compromise ended the serious crisis. Russia received central Poland, Austria retained her Polish possessions, Cracow became a free city, and Prussia was granted a broad girdle of Polish territories east of the Oder connect-

* Gerhard: *England und der Aufstieg Russlands,* pp. 417 ff.

ing Silesia with northern Pomerania and East Prussia. Prussia held Danzig and the lower Vistula valley, in our own day usually called the Polish Corridor, as a bridge to East Prussia.

Definite barriers were thereby erected against further Russian expansion toward the west. Russia had, of course, won additional land in the historic Europe and in this fourth partition of Poland had thwarted any likelihood of restoring a kingdom of Poland that was not under Russian tutelage. On the other hand, the eastern frontiers of Austria and Prussia gave the two central European states defensive military positions that, though not absolutely superior, were strong enough to deter Russia from crossing the lines for the next century (except when by invitation of the Vienna Government a Russian army in 1849 went into Hungary to assist in subduing the Hungarian revolution). Castlereagh and Metternich were thus successful in removing the Russian army from western and central Europe as well as in cutting down the prize that Russia had hoped for in eastern Europe. Russia was the first power that came to feel the strength of the restored European balance of power, and she had to retreat before it.

It was natural that with the growing tension between Britain and Austria on one side, and Russia and Prussia on the other, France would gain in political stature. The victorious four powers had not, of course, intended to give France a major voice in the peace settlement, and the quick revival of French political influence is often ascribed to the uncanny diplomatic ability of Talleyrand. It is true that he was a superb diplomatist, and his activities will always be admired by the student of diplomatic history. But the fundamental decision that France was to be continued as one of the great powers of Europe had been made without him, and all that he did was to make it immediately effective in the French interest.

Napoleon's return from Elba and the Hundred Days again brought France under a cloud of suspicion and destroyed much of what Talleyrand had achieved by his subtle and bold diplomacy. France was not fully admitted to the Concert of Europe before 1818. But one may question the wisdom of some of Talleyrand's moves prior to Napoleon's return. He was largely responsible for the decision of the powers to deny Prussia the annexation of Saxony. By the preservation of one of the middle-sized German states, he and Metternich thought they would gain an additional guarantee against a Prussian attempt at the unification of Germany. It was a doubtful gain for French diplomacy, however, for, though Prussia could annex only one third of Saxony, she was given instead the Rhineland, chiefly because the British wanted a strong military power at the middle Rhine.

Prussia seemed to be weakened after 1815 owing to the fact that her territories were broken up in two separate parts; the eastern lands of the monarchy, composed of Brandenburg, the new Saxon acquisitions, Silesia, Posnania, Pomerania, and Eastern Prussia were separated from Westphalia and the Rhineland in the west by Hanover, Hesse, and other German states. In reality the Vienna treaty made Prussia into the strongest of the German states. Before 1806 Prussia had looked to the east, and if Russia had not pressed her back after 1812, she might have developed, not into a multinational, but into a binational state in eastern Europe resembling Austria. Indeed, in 1806 every third subject of the Prussian crown was a Pole. But with the acquisition of the Rhineland in 1815 Prussia straddled all of northern Germany from Aachen to Tilsit and became the major German state on the Rhine, the real link between north and south Germany; naturally she desired to bridge the separated eastern and western sections of the monarchy and acquired a profound interest in the economic and political unification of Germany.

Austria's refusal to resume her former position along the Rhine, not to speak of the Austrian Netherlands, promoted the reorientation of Prussian policy. He who guarded the Rhine was inevitably viewed as the protagonist of the German national cause. Metternich knew this and

wanted Austria to return to the Rhine, but he was overruled by those Austrian groups that thought of the future
Austria as a compact southeastern European power. However, the policy of concentrating Austrian possessions
around Vienna, Prague, Budapest, Venice, and Milan did
not take cognizance of the responsibilities that Austria had
assumed in ruling Germany and Italy through federative
policies. The Austrian position in Europe thus could be
challenged both on the basis of principle and actual power.

But in spite of the uncertainties introduced by its central
European provisions the Vienna settlement created a European political system whose foundations lasted for a full
century. For a hundred years there occurred no wars of
world-wide scope like those of the twenty-odd years after
1792. Europe experienced frightful wars, particularly between 1854 and 1878, but none of them was a war in
which all the European states or even all the great European powers participated. The European wars of the nineteenth century produced shifts of power, but they were
shifts within the European political system and did not upset that system as such.

2. THE CONCERT OF EUROPE, 1815–50

THE peace settlement of Vienna has more of-
ten been condemned than praised. The accusation most fre-
quently levelled against the Congress of Vienna has been
that it lacked foresight in appraising the forces of modern
nationalism and liberalism. Foresight is, indeed, one of the
main qualities that distinguishes the statesman from the
mere political professional. But even a statesman can only
build with the bricks at hand and cannot hope to construct
the second floor before he has modelled the first by which
to shelter his own generation. His foresight of future developments can often express itself only by cautious at-

tempts at keeping the way open for an evolution of the new forces.

It is questionable how successful the Congress of Vienna was in this respect. None of the Congress representatives was a statesman or political thinker of the first historic rank. All of them were strong partisans of conservatism or outright reaction, and they found the rectitude of their convictions confirmed by the victory of the old powers over the revolutionary usurper. Still, they did not make a reactionary peace. They recognized that France could not live without a constitutional charter, and they knew, too, that the Holy Roman Empire was beyond resurrection. The new German Confederation represented a great improvement of the political conditions of Germany if one remembers that in Germany as well as in Italy the national movements were not strong enough to serve as pillars of a new order. In eastern Europe, furthermore, the modern ideas of nationality had hardly found more than a small academic and literary audience. A peace treaty cannot create new historical forces; it can only place the existing ones in a relationship most conducive to the maintenance of mutual confidence and least likely to lead to future conflict. The rest must be left to the ever continuing and never finished daily work of statesmen.

In this light the Vienna settlement was a constructive peace treaty. Its chief authors, Castlereagh, Metternich, Alexander I, and Hardenberg, had a very inadequate vision of the ideas and forces that were to dominate the nineteenth century, but they had clear notions about the vital necessity of establishing an equilibrium among the powers that determined the political life of Europe. They had carefully directed the war efforts of their countries with this necessity in mind and were able to create such an equilibrium in the Peace of Vienna.

The statesmen of Vienna, however, believed that it was not enough merely to revive the eighteenth century balance of power. The experience of common danger, shared by all the European states in the years between 1792 and 1815, would, it was thought, persuade the states to look at the balance of power less as a means for the advancement of their selfish interests than as the foundation of concerted action for the general welfare of the European community. These expectations were only partly fulfilled, but they were no idle and quickly forgotten dreams. During the early part of the nineteenth century the sharp conflicts of power were mitigated by a sense of European responsibility. And even when wars and national revolutions had put this to a hard test after the middle of the century, a common European consciousness survived.

But the victorious powers failed in 1814–15 and in the years thereafter to create international institutions that embodied these principles. The Congress of Aachen of 1818 codified the diplomatic rules among states, which had been vague before. This code, however, was helpful only in a technical sense and did not solve problems of political substance. The sovereignty of states remained unimpaired. An attempt was made to transform the balance-of-power system into some sort of federation of the four or, after the readmission of France, five big powers. The Concert of Europe, through regular meetings of the monarchs or their leading ministers, was to settle the controversial political issues. Four such conferences were held between 1818 and 1822 at Aachen, Troppau, Laibach, and Verona, but the nascent confederation of Europe broke down, since the social and political objectives of the five powers could not be unified.

The breach occurred over the question of whether or not the guarantee of the Vienna settlement by the five powers should extend to the preservation of the monarchical governments that had been restored in 1815. Metternich and Alexander I were afraid of revolution. The rise of Napoleon, in their opinion, had been the result of the French Revolution and the demonic forces that it had set loose. The European equilibrium was dependent on the stability of the social and political order of Europe. They urged, therefore, that the powers that formed the five-power system, the so-called pentarchy, should intervene wherever internal revolution threatened the "legitimate" order. Britain, on the other hand, even before the reform of 1832, felt differently. Social and political change did not frighten British statesmen, who knew already that the new forces could not be submerged, but could only be guided and channelled.

It is doubtful, nevertheless, whether Canning would have announced non-intervention as the principle of British foreign policy if the issue had not been one of overseas interests. Actually he agreed to giving France a temporary mandate for her intervention in Spain, provided she would not attack England's ally Portugal and would abstain from the attempt to restore the Latin American colonies to Spanish control. It was on the seas that Britain was supreme and the continental monarchies powerless. The unchallengeable British command of the sea cut off the states of the European continent from any major political influence in the Western hemisphere. Whereas in the eighteenth century the Americas were a battleground in the wars of the European powers, or at least one of the prizes at stake, after 1815 the Western hemisphere enjoyed an insular character. Britain did not, of course, thereby gain sole predominance in the New World. New opportunities opened before the United States that were boldly seized in the declarations of the Monroe Doctrine in 1823. Canning's famous dictum that he called in the New World to redress the balance of the Old was a boastful statement that will not stand up to any historical analysis. The United States had no intention of contributing to balancing the Old World nor was American policy under the guidance of the British Government. But Canning's remarks illustrate the British consciousness of the fact that, though Britain needed the European balance of power, she could hope to defy the rest of Europe in regions in which her own sea-power was dominant.

The principles of intervention and non-intervention did not express the realities of this conflict between Britain and the other major powers. Britain had already intervened in Greece and in Portugal, where it suited her interest. Non-intervention and intervention began to mean one and the same thing, namely protection of the government that the British cabinet favored for economic or political reasons, either by the indirect method of blocking the intervention of other foreign powers or by direct British assistance. Under Palmerston this policy assumed a more ideological tinge; once the French deserted the cause of legitimacy in 1830 and British policy could make itself even more strongly felt on the Continent, Britain became the champion of constitutional government everywhere. There still remained a great difference between the British advocacy of liberal and national reforms and the actual conduct of British foreign policy. Palmerston showed, for example, small interest in the national movement in Germany, while the close Anglo-Turkish relations during this period were not adversely affected by the steady failure of reform in Turkey.

Metternich's conception of a European political system resting upon the balance of power among the five major states, who would act in concert to maintain both international "tranquillity" and internal "stability," could not be realized. Metternich has gained in historical stature, since modern historians have refused to view him through the glasses of his nineteenth century liberal foes. He showed great strength in the heroic years of his career, 1812–15, in his inflexible determination to achieve a revival of the balance of power. But his confidence that the new Concert of Europe could make the social and political processes of western Europe and possibly the whole world stand still or even retrogress showed the limits of his political realism. He had no understanding of the dynamic forces that the industrial revolution in England had produced in his own lifetime. We know now that his advice in foreign policy was often overruled by the Austrian Emperor and his counsel on internal Austrian affairs often rejected. It is still true, however, that even in terms of Austrian self-interest his policy of international and internal conservatism was a temporary, not a constructive, solution.

Although Metternich's program did not become the ruling principle of the political life of the whole of Europe after 1815, it was accepted by Russia and Prussia, in part because political conditions in these countries favored it. Metternich convinced the Czar of the deadly dangers of liberalism, and Alexander's mysticism and the sudden recognition of the revolutionary movement in his own empire forced him even more strongly into the reactionary camp. In Prussia, too, the social and political forces were favorable to a reactionary course. After the defeat by Napoleon in 1806–07, it is true, Prussian reformers like Baron Stein, Hardenberg, Humboldt, Scharnhorst, and Gneisenau had begun to imbue the state of Frederick the Great, which was an obedient machine in the hands of the monarch, with the spirit of free individual initiative and proud citizenship. They had wished in particular to have the middle classes participate in the management of public affairs, since these groups represented the new economic enterprise and the new national culture that had grown up in the age of Kant and Goethe. Prussia was to become not only the Germanic model state but also the active protagonist of German national unity. This policy had contributed greatly to the revival of Prussian power and thereby to the downfall of Napoleon, but Prussia had played only a modest role at the Congress of Vienna. However, the Prussian reforms of 1807 and 1815 had not reached their ultimate goals. They had still to be crowned and made secure by the grant of a general popular representation. But once the Prussian state was out of jeopardy the old social groups pressed their claims for predominance with fresh vigor. The Prussian gentry—or *Junkers*—and the closely allied reactionary elements of the civilian and military bureaucracy could impose their will on the timid King Frederick William III. Plans for a constitution and other reforms were shelved after 1819, and Prussia became an autocratic and bureaucratic monarchy. The most important leaf that the Prussian reformers had taken from the book of the French Revolution, universal military service of all able-bodied citizens, was retained as the only means by which Prussia could hope to maintain an extraordinary military establishment. But, although the Prussian reformers had intended to use the new military system for the defeat of Napoleonic France, they had wanted it also as a means for spreading political responsibility among the various classes of Prussia. In the period after 1819 the professional officer corps, mostly composed of *Junkers*, were able to frustrate the transformation of the royal army into a citizens' force.

The re-establishment of conservative control over Prussia's army did not mean the strengthening of Prussian tendencies to be aggressive in international politics. On the contrary, the Prussian army did not fight in a foreign war for the next half-century, whereas all the other major powers of Europe were involved in various international conflicts. The conservative rulers of Prussia after 1819 realized that a policy that aimed at the unification of Germany under Prussian leadership required further liberalization of the Prussian monarchy. They preferred the preservation of their social privileges to the aggrandizement of Prussia. Prussia became a faithful supporter of the Vienna settlement and of the doctrines of international conservatism. Only the foreign economic policy of Prussia continued in a liberal and national direction. The Prusso-German *Zollverein* of 1834, which created a customs union between Prussia and the most important central and southern German states, was a great step in the direction that Bismarck was to follow thirty years later.

Metternich's plans for Europe became guiding principles only in the policy of these three eastern European powers. Their governments had a common interest in the suppression of the liberal and national movements that were to them an equal threat to their international and domestic safety. Austria instigated and originally led the eastern group, but as Britain and, somewhat later, France placed themselves in growing opposition to the eastern monarchies, it was inevitable that the strongest and least assailable among them should become prominent. Czar Nicholas I took full advantage of Russia's dominant position. The cause of Russian czardom was fortified by the existence of these two conservative and antinationalist governments in central Europe, which served as a buffer against the impact of western European liberalism and as a guarantee against the national upheavals in Russia's western possessions, among which Poland naturally caused the greatest trouble.

Czar Nicholas did not hesitate to use the Russian power to intervene in the central European revolutions of 1848–9 and to dictate the full restoration of the *status quo ante* in central Europe. Against the onslaught of liberal and national movements the Austrian monarchy defended itself successfully in Italy, Bohemia, and Austria proper, but it failed to subdue the Hungarian revolution. The dispatch of a Russian army to Hungary brought the decision and restored, temporarily at least, the conservative Habsburg monarchy. Thereafter Russia and Austria combined to restore the old order of Germany. Prussia had made few concessions to liberalism and to the German national movement, but after the collapse of the revolution tried to strengthen the federal union of the German states. Faced with the stern resistance of Austria and Russia she had to beat a full retreat and accept at Olmütz in 1850 the complete revival of the effete German Confederation.

The Russian intervention in central Europe in 1849–50 dealt a hard and in some respects crippling blow to the rising liberal forces in the Habsburg empire, Germany, and Italy. It would be erroneous to ascribe the weaknesses and failures of the liberalism of this region during the hundred years after 1850 exclusively or even primarily to the actions of Nicholas I, but there is more than a superficial connection between the present-day Russian antiliberal intervention and that of the Czars.

During the half-century after the Congress of Vienna, Europe divided into two groups, the Two and the Three as

Palmerston called them, and their differences were hardened by the conflict of ideologies. Still, Europe was not split completely. Britain and Russia, standing at opposite ends, did co-operate at times—in the liberation of Greece, for instance, when they acted together without and against Austria. Prussia, who was on the whole a loyal member of the eastern group, tended to favor the West in economic policy. Austria, on the other hand, found herself ever so often at odds with Russia over the Near Eastern question. France and Britain had their *ententes cordiales*, but they also had periodic conflicts, chiefly over colonial and Mediterranean problems. For, although France could not hope to resume the hundred years' war for colonial supremacy that had come to a close in 1815, she pressed her colonial claims energetically.

Since every European power continued to think of all the others as integral partners in a political system that guaranteed its own survival, the contrast between the western and eastern powers led to collisions but not to the breakup of the European political system as such. Even the ideological conflict was not altogether an element of division. The monarchs had been the first to speak of their solidarity beyond the frontiers of their states and to act accordingly, and it is not surprising that the opposition to the monarchical conservatism of the age of restoration organized itself on an international level. Liberals supported each other over the barriers of state boundaries, and the champions of nationality felt a similar comradeship. There were men who fought in the Latin American revolutions, in Greece, in the Polish Revolution of 1830, and again in the central European revolutions of 1848. The army brought together by the German democrats, who attempted to save some of the achievements of the revolution in the Baden revolt of 1849, was commanded by one of these international fighters for liberty, a Polish general.

As the monarchs banded together against what they indiscriminately called *the* revolution, so the liberal and national movements maintained mutual contacts. The liberals were correct in their judgment that the progress of the causes of nationality and freedom in central and eastern Europe depended to a large extent on the breakdown of the alliance of the eastern rulers. The monarchs on their part realized that if they weakened each other by a war comparable in size to the Napoleonic wars they would open the gates to their own internal destruction. The awareness of this fact was one of the forces holding the eastern alliance together. The internationalism of the political philosophy of Karl Marx and Friedrich Engels was a true child of this age of international political and ideological fronts. These men were, of course, also fierce opponents of Russian czardom, and Friedrich Engels, the military brain of the early Marxist school, was mapping plans for removing Russia's pernicious influence from Europe as the first step in the preparation for the coming social revolution.*

* Cf. S. Neumann: "Engels und Marx: Military Concepts of the Social Revolutionaries," in E. M. Earle (ed.): *Makers of Modern Strategy* (Princeton: 1943), pp. 155~71.

III

EUROPE IN THE AGE OF

NATIONALISM AND IMPERIALISM

1. EUROPE AND THE RISE OF THE GERMAN EMPIRE

THE internationalism of Europe's crowned heads and liberal parties, which was so conspicuous in the 1850's, began to fade rather quickly. The national movements of the early nineteenth century had been largely animated by the belief, most clearly expounded by Mazzini, that once the nations could create free governments of their own choice and could realize the highest aspirations of their national cultures, the international conflicts would wither away and a brotherly federation of nations would come into existence. It is this liberal version of nationalism that was still reflected in Woodrow Wilson's political philosophy. But, though the realization of the principle of national self-determination could have resolved some and eased other tensions of Europe, it is questionable whether it could ever have served by itself as a workable basis of a European peace organization.

The French Revolution had proclaimed the democratic national idea as the ideal that would bring happiness to all humanity, and its romantic counterpart, the cultural nationalism of Herder, aimed also at the welfare of humanity rather than of a single nation. But the French Revolution, no doubt largely in defense against the military in-

tervention of the absolutistic states, had proceeded to transform the idea of nationality into an instrument of French
expansion. And on the other side of the Rhine, German
nationalism, which developed in reaction to the French invasion and Napoleonic domination, tended to disregard
cosmopolitan ends. The original liberal aims of nationalism
were easily neglected for the sake of power, and this neglect increased in Germany after the defeat of the national
and liberal revolutions of 1848. On the other hand, in
Italy at this time, the narrow selfishness latent in nationalism presented no such burning issue, since she had always
enjoyed the support of the western powers and could never
hope to accomplish her national unification except in close
alliance with other nations.

In contrast to the Italian, the German national movement
had no friends in Europe; the West looked at it coldly,
the East was actively hostile. Prussia, the only German
state that could have assumed a role analogous to that of
Piedmont in Italy, refused to promote the German national cause out of a fear that she might lose her conservative authoritarian character. It was in Germany, consequently, that the liberals after 1850 radically questioned
the practical political value of a liberal ideology. Not
ideas, but only power could bring about unification, and the
German liberals had to choose between unity or liberty if
they did not wish to miss both forever. They chose the
program then named *Realpolitik.** Their choice was an
event of far-reaching consequences in the world of ideas.

More immediately important than the incipient disintegration of the liberal ideology in central Europe was the
change in the policies of the European governments after
the revolutions of 1848. Almost all of them displayed a
new cocky selfishness. The Austria of Prince Schwarzenberg, which had just been saved from disintegration by

---

* The word became popular through the publication of A. L. von
Rochau's *Grundsätze der Realpolitik angewendet auf die staatlichen
Zustände Deutschlands* (1853). The book had a great influence on
the young Treitschke.

Russia's intervention in the Hungarian revolution, did not hide her sympathy for the Anglo-French attempt at closing the Near East to Russia in the Crimean War of 1854. Schwarzenberg had not hesitated to accept Russian assistance in subduing the national and liberal movements of central Europe, but once the autocratic Government in Vienna was in the saddle again it was anxious to demonstrate that it was a stronger champion of Austrian interests than the liberals or independent nationalities could ever hope to be. In other words, the horse began to dominate the rider.

In Metternich's days a society dominated by the gentry had tried to stabilize its power by international friendships, but now the cold wind of the modern class struggle forced the old aristocratic societies to recognize the strength of other social groups. Broadly speaking, one may say that in all the continental countries affected by the revolutions of the mid-century the autocratic governments survived because they rallied to their support the old classes of the agrarian society, the peasants and artisans. Yet all the restored governments felt that the new *bourgeoisie* had to be given some satisfaction. The autocratic governments refused to have the *bourgeoisie* participate in the formulation of policy but attempted to take the wind out of the sails of nationalism and liberalism by trying to realize some of the political and economic aims of the middle class.

This new situation created by the growth of the industrial society was highlighted by the rise of the dictatorship of Louis Bonaparte after the Revolution of 1848. He made himself the master of France by mobilizing the peasants to whom he tried to add the industrial workers. Universal suffrage was the means by which both groups were to be activated against the liberal *bourgeoisie*. Once Napoleon III had gained supremacy, however, he began to woo the *bourgeoisie*. His economic policies boosted its power, while his foreign policy played up to its national pride. But, just as Austria's policy during the Crimean War had broken up the alliance of the three eastern monarchies, or at least had induced Russia to extend her favor to Prussia rather

than Austria, so Napoleon's foreign and colonial policies
in the second decade of his rule led to the breakup of
the entente of the western powers. During the 1850's
France and Britain fought together against Russia in the
Crimean War. The French-Italian war against Austria in
1859 was not opposed by Britain, which in a way derived
the credit for bringing on the ultimate unification of Italy
by supporting the Italian revolution. But when France
subsequently became increasingly active in the Levant and
also intervened in Mexico, Britain grew uneasy. Special
anxiety was felt over the expansion of the French navy,
which the British found difficult to meet when the tran-
sition from the wooden to the iron-clad vessel had temporarily deprived Britain of her head start.*

The deep rifts that appeared both in the alliance of the
three eastern courts and in the western entente during the
fifties and sixties of the nineteenth century disrupted the
working of the European concert of powers. It was weakened further by the relatively disinterested attitude that its
most powerful members, Britain and Russia, assumed in
these years towards European problems. Russia had been
thrown by the Crimean War into an internal crisis, and
the domestic reforms culminating in the liberation of the
Russian peasants absorbed her energies for a long time.
Britain receded to the sidelines later than Russia; as she
began to feel concern over the consequences of her irreso-
lute policy with regard to the American Civil War, and after her attempts to intervene in the Polish revolution of
1863 and the Danish war of 1864 proved futile, she realized more or less clearly that she could not hope to intervene successfully in European affairs without continental
allies. For the next decade "non-intervention" was the
vaunted principle of British foreign policy, but it was
chiefly a slogan to cover the British retreat and British
isolation rather than a bold challenge to the other pow-

* Sir H. Richmond: *Statesmen and Sea Power* (2nd ed., Oxford:
1947), pp. 267 ff.

ers and a device to re-establish British influence as it had been in Canning's days.

With the two powers at Prussia's eastern and western peripheries keeping aloof from Europe, the stage was set for Bismarck. His policies were not a mere emulation of Napoleon III's tactics, but nobody had studied Bonapartistic schemes as seriously as this Prussian *Junker*. Bismarck took the helm of the Prussian state at the moment when the monarchy was ready to surrender to the rising tide of liberalism. Bismarck's supreme objective was the perpetuation of the dominant role of the crown and of the social forces allied with it. He felt that with the unbroken tradition of the state of Frederick the Great behind him he could employ Bonapartistic devices with better results than the revolutionary upstart Napoleon. Furthermore, the strength and mobility of the Prussian army was superior to that of any other European army. Bismarck, like Napoleon III, believed that an autocratic government could hold its own as long as it enjoyed the full support of the old agrarian classes possibly augmented by the assistance of such new antiliberal forces as the industrial workers. He trusted that the political aspirations of the liberals could be deflated if a conservative government boldly realized those liberal aims that were compatible with the continuation of an autocratic regime. National unification proved to be the solution.

At the beginning of his political ministry Bismarck bluntly proclaimed that German unity could not be brought about "by speeches and majority resolutions" but only "by blood and iron." In these words he rejected the political program of the German liberals who hoped to attract the south German liberals into a union with Prussia by turning Prussia into a liberal state. But Bismarck's clarion call implied also a criticism of the spineless policy during the 1850's of the Prussian conservatives, who had failed to take advantage of the opportunities that had offered themselves for establishing an assertive and egotistical Prussia. Bismarck proposed to play for high stakes. He wanted to solve the problem of German unification by the military defeat of Austria and the transformation of the Prussian Customs Union into a German federal state. At the same time the achievement of national unity through the military strength of an absolute Prussia was to be the death of the political ambitions of the liberal movement.

From 1862 to 1866 Bismarck defied the liberal majority in the Prussian parliament and used all the devices of absolutism, such as rule without an approved budget and censorship of the press, to suppress the liberal movement. Simultaneously, with Austria as an unenthusiastic partner he used the Prussian army to satisfy popular national aspirations in Schleswig-Holstein. Then he expanded the conflict between Austria and Prussia over the settlement of the Schleswig-Holstein issue into the war of 1866 for the supremacy of Germany.* The battle of Sadowa and the subsequent Peace of Prague excluded Austria from a new union of German states in which the southern German states were joined to the North German Confederation by military alliances and the Customs Union. But Bismarck's provocations and the clumsy and overbearing attitude of Napoleon III led to the Franco-Prussian War of 1870–1, in the course of which the North German Confederation was transformed into a German empire under Prussian leadership.

The achievement of German unity gave Bismarck the power to force the German liberals to decide whether they were more eager to see unity or liberty achieved in Germany. The majority of them proved willing to compromise with Bismarck. Since centralization went rather far under the new constitution he needed the liberal movement to some extent to counterbalance the particularistic German forces represented chiefly by the German princes. The constitution of the new German empire was, therefore, a bit

* Cf. the author's article "Moltke and Schlieffen" in Earle (ed.): *Makers of Modern Strategy*, pp. 172–205.

more centralized and more liberal than Bismarck wished, but he maintained control of the crucial policy-making positions. No decisive power over military and foreign affairs by the constituted popular bodies was allowed in the second German empire. Bismarck made all sorts of concessions in the field of social and economic reform but was absolutely adamant with regard to the powers of the parliament. The direction of foreign and military matters remained a privilege of the Crown.

The pseudo-constitutional character of the new German empire was even more accentuated when in 1878 Bismarck decided to give up free trade and imposed a policy protecting the interests of the Prussian *Junker* agrarians against the importation of cheap Russian and American grain while at the same time introducing tariffs benefiting the growing German iron industries. Just as in 1866 and 1871 the German liberals had had to sacrifice the core of their political faith, so they were forced to jettison the major part of their economic program after 1878. The leading industrial groups of German society readily accepted a protectionist trade policy, and the unity of the liberal *bourgeoisie* crumbled. Thirty years after German liberalism had burst into existence in the Revolution of 1848, it ceased to be an independent political movement. Thereafter the majority of the German *bourgeoisie*, if they did not, like the higher *bourgeoisie*, become absolute supporters of the regime, were driven to further concession and compromise. The appearance of a powerful socialist workers' movement extinguished the last remaining fervor for reform among the liberal *bourgeoisie* and made them take cover under the wings of the established government. The second German empire was founded "by blood and iron" and socially stabilized by "iron and grain." For more than fifty years the German political scene was overshadowed by the alliance of the "barons of the halm" and the "barons of the smokestack," who maintained the army and bureaucracy in power.

Bismarck's policy is often called *Realpolitik* in the sense that it was not motivated by ideological principles and merely executed what the realities of the political situation demanded. But this interpretation of Bismarck's statesmanship is erroneous. No doubt Bismarck had a keenly realistic sense of the forces with which he was dealing. He was an accomplished diplomatic tactician who knew how to shift his ground or argument as well as how to delay or disguise. But, although Bismarck was not given to ideological bigotry, he held strong political and social convictions that guided all his actions. This Prussian *Junker* believed wholeheartedly in monarchy and the superiority of a military and bureaucratic regime tempered by a certain amount of public discussion. By his war policies between 1864 and 1871 he wanted to make Prussia strong in Europe and respected by the German people. In breaking up the German liberal movement and compelling the German *bourgeoisie* to resign itself to a semi-absolutistic monarchy with some liberal trimmings he assumed he had shattered future internal opposition.

This policy cannot be called *Realpolitik,* for it was colored by strong ideological beliefs. A less conservative statesman might have wondered whether Germany would not grow stronger by giving the new classes a full share in carrying out the responsibilities of government. He might also have argued that excessive use of force was bound to undermine the regard for law and lawful procedures on which a healthy national and international community life is based. Was there ever more than a temporary halt to coercion in the Bismarckian system? In 1890, before his resignation as chancellor, he even proposed to suspend his own constitution of 1867-71 and to impose a new one that would have disenfranchised the German workers. Yet he never succeeded after 1871 in stemming the growth of the Social Democratic movement in spite of his suppressive measures coupled with a paternalistic social legislation.

But there was another side to Bismarck's statesmanship, which contributed greatly to restoring the Concert of Europe to some working order. Bismarck was neither a Napoleon I nor a Hitler bent upon conquering all of Europe. He considered the continued existence of a system of balance among the five great powers as natural and necessary. He made every effort to maintain Austria as a great European power. If Bismarck had been a nationalist, he would have pressed the Prussian victory in the hope of bringing the German-Austrians, then or later, into his new empire. But Bismarck as monarchist and European diplomat was well satisfied to leave ten million Germans outside the German empire in order to neutralize thirty million southeastern Europeans. He feared that if a great power did not guard the Danube valley, Russia would find the gate of central Europe open. Co-operation between the new Germany and Austria-Hungary was to him a vital concern, and immediately after Sadowa he began to make every effort toward an early restoration of close relations between the two central powers.

The Franco-German settlement of 1871 did not rest on the same objectivity of judgment. Bismarck never contemplated the destruction of France as one of the big five of Europe. But he considered Franco-German political enmity as a permanent element of past and future history. He therefore did not hesitate to wound France and keep her in a state of instability and isolation. The annexation of Alsace against the will of its population was further aggravated by Moltke's demand for French-speaking parts of Lorraine including the fortress city of Metz, to which Bismarck reluctantly assented. For Bismarck was fully aware that the annexation of Strasbourg and Alsace could be justified, not in terms of national self-determination, but chiefly on strategic grounds that then were equally applicable to Metz and Lorraine. The Peace of Frankfurt thus altered the balance between Germany and France in a drastic fashion. And it was a sign of great European insecurity that the change of the Franco-German frontier, which had been agreed upon by all the European powers at the Congress of Vienna as one of the cornerstones of European peace, could be unilaterally imposed without being drawn before a council of powers. Gladstone thought of intervening, but England was isolated and, even worse, at loggerheads with Russia, which had used this moment to free herself of some of the shackles that the western European powers had placed on her capacity for expansion in the Near East.

Bismarck took the Franco-German conflict for granted but did not think that Germany, once she had gained an ideal military frontier against France, would have to feel too seriously concerned. France could become a threat to Germany only if she succeeded in finding allies ready to support her in *revanche*. It was the chancellor's major aim to block any such attempt. He threw his support behind the Third Republic and against a monarchical restoration, because a French monarchy might have found it possible to form an alliance with Russia and perhaps even with Russia and Austria, a return of that dreaded alliance that Prince Kaunitz, Maria Theresa's chancellor, had brought together against Frederick the Great in 1756.

Yet protective measures were not the major devices in Bismarck's diplomatic armory. His chief positive endeavor was to tie the two other great continental powers to Germany. The most exposed frontier of Germany was her eastern frontier; the most dangerous threat to German unity was a renewal of the struggle for German hegemony between Austria and Prussia. These were good reasons of *Realpolitik*, but even here we find Bismarck injecting his ideological convictions. In his *Reminiscences and Reflections*, which can be called his political testament, he summed up the supreme objective of his foreign policy after 1871 as aiming at the closest co-operation between the three emperors and later, possibly, the king of Italy. These powers should direct their alliance, he wrote, "toward the imminent struggle between the two European movements which Napoleon called the republican and the kossack. In present terms I would define them on one hand as the system of order on a monarchical basis and on the other as the social republic, a level to which the antimonarchical development sinks slowly or suddenly until the insufferable nature of the ensuing conditions makes the disillusioned people receptive to a forcible return to monarchical institutions of a Caesarist type," and he added the warning: "If the monarchical governments do not understand the need for working together in the interest of political and social order but instead surrender to the chauvinistic sentiments of their subjects, I fear that the international revolutionary and social struggles, which we shall have to fight through, will become more dangerous and more unpropitious for a victory of the monarchical order."*

Bismarck hoped to be able to keep the three emperors together if Germany renounced all expansionist aims. With a phrase borrowed from Metternich's vocabulary he declared that the German Empire was "satiated" and would use its power exclusively for the furtherance of general peace. In his days the greatest threat to European peace was the Near Eastern question, since it brought both Britain and Austria into conflict with Russia. It was here then that Germany, which in Bismarck's opinion had no interests of her own in the Balkans or Asia Minor, could exercise her influence in a manner most profitable to her own general safety and to the cause of international peace.

In bare outline, Bismarck's policy consisted in assuring Russia of Germany's benevolent neutrality with regard to any Russian moves in the Near East while keeping her apprised of Germany's determination to assist Austria-Hungary in case of a direct Russian attack. Vienna was simultaneously informed that, while Germany would protect the present position of Austria-Hungary, she would not support her in a Balkan policy that would meet with Russian opposition. Bismarck had originally expected that some agreement could be found by which the Turkish Straits and the eastern Balkans would become a Russian sphere, while

* O. von Bismarck: *Erinnerung und Gedanke,* critical edition by G. Ritter and R. Stadelmann (Berlin: 1932), p. 398 [my translation].

the western part would be an Austrian domain. But when it was proved impossible to attain such an accord, Bismarck suggested that Austria's natural ally in the pursuit of an active Balkan policy was Britain.

Bismarck's policy fell short of what Russia thought she could expect in return for her tolerant attitude toward the German unification by Prussia. Governments have always been inclined to turn sins of omission into virtues of commission. Russia was now faced with a power in the West far more independent than either the old Austria or Prussia, not to mention the German Confederation, had been. Bismarck, it is true, had crushed liberalism in central Europe and had thereby kept intact the ideological security belt to the west of Russia; but Russians could question whether they had gained much by the fact that Bismarck's Germany took a friendlier view of Russian expansion in the Near East than Austria had done in the past. Russia had still to counter British opposition strengthened by Austria-Hungary, and she could not meet Austria's resistance head-on owing to Germany's declared interest in Austria's European position.

It was not surprising, therefore, that the Russian nationalists soon exclaimed that the way to Constantinople led through the Brandenburg Gate. However, Czars Alexander II and Alexander III were never seriously tempted to consider taking this road. On the whole one may doubt whether the official Russian foreign policy was deeply and genuinely motivated by Panslavist ideas. The uppermost concern of the court and the Russian bureaucracy was the preservation of the Czarist empire and its existing political and social structure. It was well recognized that Russia by herself could not hope to defeat Germany and that a fight between the two major monarchies would lead to revolution. Nevertheless, although the Czars were absolutistic rulers, their will was no longer absolute. Most of the downtrodden Russian people were without a voice. The politically active and vocal groups were divided into revolutionary and nationalistic factions. Consequently, it was imperative for the Czarist Government to pay special heed to the nationalists—those groups of the *bourgeoisie* and intelligentsia that accepted the monarchy as a symbol and means of nationalistic expansion. Czardom was, of course, most anxious to strengthen its social basis at times when over-exertions had weakened the hold of the Government— after the Russo-Turkish War of 1877-8, for instance, or after the Russo-Japanese War of 1904–05. Russian nationalism and Panslavism, therefore, were a force in Russian policy more for internal than external reasons.

Bismarck's Three Emperors League came into being in 1872-3 but lasted only to 1876, when the Near Eastern crises, finally resulting in the Russo-Turkish War of 1877-8, broke up the close relationship. The menace of Russian control over the Turkish Straits and the Balkans induced Disraeli to dispatch British naval forces to Constantinople. Together with Austria, Britain vigorously opposed the crippling Treaty of San Stefano that Russia forced upon Turkey. The mediating role assumed by Bismarck contributed very greatly to Europe's escape from a repetition of the Crimean War. The Congress of Berlin of 1878 demonstrated that the formation of the new German empire had added to European security.

But the Congress of Berlin, by cutting down Russia's military gains, which she would have been incapable of defending in a war against Britain and Austria, caused profound Russian resentment against the key position of Germany in European affairs. The fulminations and acts of intimidation emanating from Russia led Bismarck to conclude the German-Austrian alliance of 1879, a mutual defense pact against Russian aggression. In Bismarck's opinion the alliance did not signify an option of Austria against Russia, but served only as a drastic reminder of Germany's unshakable policy. The immediate future justified Bismarck's view. Russia became anxious to restore the Three Emperors League, which from 1881 to 1886 functioned rather well. Then a new Balkan crisis created fresh antagonism between Vienna and St. Petersburg. This time

Bismarck gave Russia a written guarantee of German diplomatic support of her claims for the Turkish Straits, the
so-called German-Russian Reinsurance Treaty of 1887. Simultaneously, however, he gave his blessing to the formation of the Mediterranean Entente, an agreement among
Britain, Austria-Hungary, and Italy for the common defense of the *status quo* in the Mediterranean. Again these
groupings produced a balance of power that preserved the
peace of Europe.

After the national revolutions and social transformations
of the mid-century had placed the continued existence of
the Concert of Europe in jeopardy, a precarious equilibrium was restored in the period between 1871 and 1890.
Still, the tremors of social and national revolts, though
subdued, remained audible in a seemingly calm political atmosphere. Bismarck was more conscious of these rum-
blings than any other statesman of the age, but he thought
that his answer to the challenge of nationalism, liberalism,
and socialism—the adoption of some aims of these movements simultaneously with the bold assertion of the supremacy of absolutistic government—set a model that the
two other imperial governments could follow.

They could do so to some extent, but Bismarck underestimated the dynamic strength of the national movements
in the Habsburg empire and of the social revolution in
Russia. It was symptomatic that at the time of the German-Russian Reinsurance Treaty a certain Alexander Ilyich
Ulyanov was executed after an abortive attempt on the
life of Alexander III, an event that proved one of the
strongest influences in the revolutionary life of the assas-
sin's younger brother Lenin, who thirty years later was to
replace the czars.* After 1867 the internal cohesion of
Austria-Hungary waned, and disintegration proceeded at an
even quicker pace after 1890. Both the Austro-Hungarian and the Russian Governments had to cope with prob-

* B. D. Wolfe: *Three Who Made a Revolution* (New York:
1948), pp. 55–66.

lems that were not entirely comparable to those of Germany.

The Three Emperors League was most stable when Russia turned her attention away from the Near East to other objectives of expansion—during the first half of the 1870's and 1880's, for instance, when she concentrated on the conquest of central Asiatic territories. It can therefore be argued that the Bismarckian policy of German-Russian friendship, subject to severe strain in the late eighties, would have become easier again after 1890, when Russia embarked on the development of her Asiatic provinces and placed great emphasis on Far Eastern affairs; for until the Russo-Japanese War of 1904-05 practically stopped Russian expansion in the Far East, Near Eastern and central Asiatic objectives remained in the background of Russian foreign policy.

Thus the change of German policy towards Russia, decided upon by Bismarck's successors when in 1890 they rejected the insistent Russian requests for the renewal of the Reinsurance Treaty, was not justified at the moment; and it lost Germany her key position in European politics. One could very well entertain serious doubts about the long-range prospects of official German-Russian amity. Bismarck himself harbored some. But a firm and mutually satisfactory understanding with Britain, the only ally who could have replaced Russia, could be achieved only so long as Germany was free to choose between a Russian and a British orientation. By the diplomatic rebuff, Russia was driven into the arms of France, and the co-operation of Germany's eastern and western neighbors developed between 1891 and 1894 into a full-fledged military alliance. Automatically the center of European politics reverted from Berlin to London. Britain now controlled the balance between two continental groups and could set the price for any favor she might extend to either of them. The Government of William II had been gravely mistaken in thinking that Germany could carry out a policy of the "free hand" without losing her predominant position in European councils. Yet under William II, Germany felt strong enough even to launch policies that directly antagonized both Russia and Britain at the same time. The creation of German interests in the Turkish empire, centering around the Bagdad railroad, ruined Russo-German relations, while the naval race caused Anglo-German hostility.

Before discussing the events that led to World War I we must look for a moment at the relationship of Germany and England during the age of Bismarck. The Chancellor thought it inconceivable that the two nations could ever go to war. But Bismarck distrusted British diplomacy for its ability to make other powers fight her wars in Europe. Germany was not to become Britain's continental sword. The cultivation of Russo-German friendship was the chief means of placing Germany on a standing of diplomatic equality. Germany's declared disinterest in the Near East was the only way to compel Britain to make a contribution of her own to the preservation of the European order. If Britain wanted to stop the Russian advance in that region, she would have to step into the breach herself.

Thus Britain was forced out of the insular aloofness into which she had retired in the 1860's. The co-operation with Austria-Hungary brought Britain at least indirectly closer to Berlin and, incidentally, completed the diplomatic isolation of France. Bismarck would have liked to have this situation spelled out in a sort of Anglo-German reinsurance treaty by which Britain would have declared her neutrality in the case of a French attack upon Germany. He wanted to take advantage not only of Anglo-Russian but also of Anglo-French tension, which found its expression in colonial rivalry.

When at the time of the Congress of Berlin Bismarck nodded assent to French plans for the acquisition of Tunisia, he hoped that French colonial expansion would alleviate French pressure at the Rhine and at the same time add fresh fuel to the competition between Britain and France. The Anglo-French colonial conflict actually became

an important, though not absolute, determinant of European politics for the next twenty-five years. And for a
short while Bismarck used this collision to make Britain
accept the founding of German colonies. These events occurred in 1884-5, at a time when the Three Emperors
League was flourishing and after Italy had joined Austria-
Hungary and Germany in the Triple Alliance of 1882.
Britain's objections to Germany's colonial claims were
countered by French and German action, co-operatively
planned, that increased British colonial difficulties—those
attending the British occupation of Egypt, for example.
Grudgingly Britain had to give ground to the new German colonial enterprise.

But Bismarck's "colonial marriage" with France was
only a passing affair. The acquisition of German colonies
was in Bismarck's eyes a desirable but not a vital aim of
German foreign policy. The reasons for his championship
of German colonial activity lay largely in domestic politics. He wanted to demonstrate, particularly to certain commercial groups but also to the German people in general,
that the new German empire was capable of satisfying
even their far-flung interests and high ambitions. The comfortable diplomatic situation of 1884-5 allowed him such
a display. Not for a moment were Bismarck's colonial
projects intended to constitute a revision of the fundamen-
tals of his continental policy. Least of all were they designs to undermine British naval or colonial supremacy
overseas. Bismarck was frank when he told British statesmen that Germany, by the acquisition of colonies, was giving Britain new hostages, since she could not hope to defend them in an emergency.

When new clouds rose on the Near Eastern horizon, Aus-
trian-Russian relations grew tense and desire for revenge
against Germany revived in France. Bismarck without any
special feeling then compromised the outstanding colonial
differences with Britain. From 1887 to the time of his
dismissal in 1890, he fought for the preservation of the
European peace along his continental defense lines. He

concluded the Reinsurance Treaty with Russia, while Salisbury built up the Mediterranean Entente with Austria-Hungary and Italy, Germany's allies through the Triple Alliance. Though Britain thereby assumed a definite commitment for the preservation of the European *status quo*, Salisbury refused to give Bismarck any binding pledge with regard to France. Obviously British freedom of action in the case of a Franco-German war was considered a valuable check on Germany, one which Britain wished to retain at least as long as Germany held back in the Near East.

Britain had watched the stormy rise of the new German empire with a concern that was felt even more keenly once British diplomats realized, after 1871, that they could no longer bypass Berlin. In the early years Bismarck was suspected of hatching schemes for the annexation of the Germanic parts of Switzerland and countries like Denmark or the Netherlands. Britain's fears soon subsided when she realized that the Bismarckian policy was no longer one of conquest. Naturally, however, Bismarck's support of Russian czardom never was popular in Britain. His restraining influence on Russian policy was not overlooked by British statesmen, but they could not forget either that his peace policy thrived on the tenseness of the political atmosphere of Europe. They were right in assuming that Bismarck was by no means interested in curing the causes of Anglo-Russian conflict and that he was equally desirous of keeping Britain and France separated. Gladstone during his ministry of 1880 aimed at a direct Anglo-Russian understanding, but failed completely. Thereafter the key position of Germany in European affairs, though not too well liked, was accepted by Britain until Germany herself relinquished it in 1890.

2. INDUSTRIAL CAPITALISM AND IMPERIALISM

CRITICAL observers of European economic life in the eighteenth century believed they detected signs of a declining vitality. Since the Renaissance, capitalism had been growing up slowly in the West, but by 1760 or so it seemed incapable of much greater expansion and possibly even to be condemned to shrink. Other historic civilizations—those of Egypt, Greece, or Rome, for instance—had advanced to economic conditions comparable to those attained in the West by the eighteenth century, but all of these civilizations had broken down or suffered steep retrogression. Actually about 1760 European capitalism was threatened by many of the scarcities that had caused the eventual decay of former civilizations. The major share of the European wealth had been acquired through colonial exploitation, but by the end of the eighteenth century many colonies had been despoiled of most of their riches —Africa had even lost much of its native population. Europe's own soil was overworked and her resources depleted. Timber, the most important raw material of the age, was getting so scarce that iron production sagged, and because of the shortage of ship-building material the expansion of overseas trade met with difficulties. The growth of population was so slow that the manpower was lacking for a vigorous development of productive forces.*

Yet this senescent Europe gave birth to a productive economy that both in form and in size has had no precedent in the history of mankind. Modern industrial capitalism raised the standard of living by 100 per cent for a population that grew two and a half times larger in the course of the nineteenth century. The industrial revolution began in Britain as early as the second half of the eighteenth century, assumed greater proportions after 1800, and moved ahead with ever increasing vigor in the 1830's

* W. Sombart: *Der moderne Kapitalismus*, Vol. II (5th ed., Munich: 1922), pp. 1137–55.

and 1840's. France, who as a result of her wars was poorer in 1815 than she had been in 1789, probably regained her former position only by 1830. The 1840's saw decisive progress toward modern capitalism in France, but the Second Empire was the true age of its establishment.

Germany at first lagged behind France. Voltaire once said that Germany was condemned to eternal poverty, and her economic development during the first half of the nineteenth century did not refute his prediction. The German national product grew between 1815 and 1848, but so did the population. The 1850's witnessed a strong spurt of capitalistic expansion, but the creation of modern German industrialism was closely interwoven with the history of the political unification of Germany after 1860. The payment of a war indemnity of five billion French francs by France in 1871-3 was an important element in the miraculous growth of German capitalism in those years, though the windfall of French gold was very ineptly used by the Germans.

The development of modern capitalism in the other European countries, such as Austria, Italy, Belgium, the Netherlands, and Scandinavia, took place at about the same time as in France and Germany, but Russia followed at a much later date. In spite of a great amount of railroad building after the 1860's, it was only after 1890 that Russia entered upon a period of more determined capitalistic and industrial expansion. But the results were small even by 1914, and the Government controlled the economy, including the distribution of foreign loans, so completely that one could argue that Russia continued to live to the end of the czarist regime under a mercantilistic system. In any event, one of the significant effects of the intensive industrialization of western and central Europe was a new accentuation of the difference between Russia and Europe.

The stormy growth of modern capitalism was checked by the severe economic crisis of 1873 followed by long years of depression and a downward trend of prices. The economic fluctuations of the next two decades were a great strain, but by 1895 the turning point had been reached, and the subsequent twenty years saw another enormous advance in economic productivity in spite of occasional, if milder, crises. Europe had reached the highest state of productive capacity when war broke out in 1914.

Did modern industrial capitalism cause the war of 1914 or at least contribute to the collapse of the European peace? This question cannot be answered simply. In the colonial wars of the eighteenth century the economic motive could be more easily grasped than in the wars of the nineteenth and twentieth centuries, in which we find far more differentiated and complex historical circumstances.

The modern industrial revolution has brought about the greatest transformation ever made in the conditions of human life. Everywhere modern capitalism, acting as the liberator from feudal bonds, aimed at the freedom of the individual, at freedom of migration, commercial interchange, and capital investment. In 1928 the eminent German historian and critic of modern capitalism Werner Sombart wrote that all the modern states, irrespective of their constitutional forms, had made the necessary arrangements in their domestic and international policies to satisfy the new capitalistic forces.* The judgment is probably too sweeping, particularly with regard to foreign policy. The liberal and democratic nations were swayed by imperialistic movements, but their political institutions proved in the long run more successful in checking them.

Although capitalism became a world-wide movement, it utterly failed to destroy nationalism. On the contrary, the capitalistic epoch became the age of nationalism above all others. Everywhere capitalism preserved and solidified the existing national states and endowed them with an infinitely greater internal and external power than they had ever owned before. To this extent modern capitalism reaffirmed the historical pattern of Europe. Furthermore, it threw the national diversity of the Continent into bold re-

* Sombart: *Der moderne Kapitalismus*, Vol. III, p. 48.

lief. Various European nations found various solutions for granting political representation to the new wealth-producing classes. In Britain the *bourgeoisie* acquired political power, and the same happened in France, but in Austria-Hungary and Germany the *bourgeoisie* did not directly share political responsibility, acting instead as a mighty pressure group on the half-absolutistic governments. There were other distinctions. Britain sacrificed her agriculture to such an extent that she became almost an exclusively industrial state, whereas Germany, in spite of her greater industrial production, managed to retain an agriculture of considerable importance. France also remained a country in which agricultural and industrial production were more evenly matched.

Capitalism also led the various states to adopt different policies in international trade. Ever after the repeal of the corn laws in 1846 Britain championed and practiced free trade. Her world-wide commercial and financial interests, together with the head start of her industries, made a policy leading to a maximum of free competitive intercourse most advantageous. British economists, especially of the Manchester school, preached that free trade was the panacea of world prosperity and world peace. Cobden believed that once political restrictions and controls had been lifted, peaceful economic dealings among peoples would supersede the political conflicts among states. For similar reasons he argued that colonies were an antiquated luxury.

The era of free trade seemed to have arrived when Cobden negotiated the Anglo-French trade treaty of 1860. Two years later the Prussian-German Customs Union concluded a liberal trade agreement with France, and other accords in western Europe followed. But Russia and Austria-Hungary —not to mention the United States—never adopted free trade, and when in 1879 Germany introduced her new iron and grain tariff, the general trend was definitely reversed. By 1896 all the continental European states had returned to protectionism. The British empire alone continued to adhere to free trade.

But, though England continued to advocate free trade, the anticolonial attitude of the "Little Englanders" like Cobden had otherwise only a passing effect on British foreign policy. With the annexation of Cyprus in 1878 and the occupation of Egypt in 1882 Britain, followed by France and Germany, entered upon a new period of colonial acquisitions. In 1876 only 10.8 per cent of the Dark Continent was dominated by Western powers; in 1900, 90.4 per cent, while the figures for the Pacific island area were 57 and 98 per cent.* Obviously the British Government believed that direct political control conferred advantages that free economic competition by itself could not gain. Trade followed the flag.

The age of free trade was only a historical interlude before the age of neo-mercantilism and imperialism. Both of the latter expressions are either vague or blurred by political controversy. In a strict sense there was no revival of mercantilism, except perhaps in Russia. Under mercantilism the manufacturer or merchant was but a servant of the state, whereas in modern times the class of financiers and industrialists can call upon governments for the protection of markets and investment opportunities.

The term "imperialism" has become even more controversial. The word originally came into usage as a description of the ambitious policies of the Second French Empire and denoted the rule of a nation-state over foreign dependent areas. In socialist and communist language, imperialism is used to define capitalism in its phase of high concentration of industrial cartels and of capital seeking new investment opportunities—"imperialism *or* the domination of the finance capital," Lenin said.† But the dogmatic assertion that finance capitalism equals imperialism should not be accepted. No doubt the desire of capitalists to find profitable investments was very important in the colonial expansion of the late nineteenth and early twentieth cen-

---

* Sombart: *Der moderne Kapitalismus*, Vol. III, p. 65.
† V. I. Lenin: *Imperialism, the Highest Stage of Capitalism* (New York: 1933).

turies, but it was by no means the exclusive cause. Strategic interests were often more important than economic interests, and the latter were highly varied. Opportunities for investment and availability of raw materials were strong incentives, but the Italians hoped also to settle surplus population, and the French had an eye on the possibilities of strengthening their war potential by the use of native manpower. In Germany certain economic interests, chiefly in Hamburg and Bremen, started the colonial development, but they represented neither the big financial nor industrial forces of German capitalism. Exports to and imports from the German colonies constituted 1 to 2 per cent of the total German trade balance.* Germany's capital investment in her colonies was small, and all these colonies were unsuitable for white settlement. The German colonies had very largely a national prestige value.

Nevertheless, capital investment was certainly of prime importance in late nineteenth century expansion. By far the largest investments were owned by Britain. In 1914 one quarter of all the British national wealth, about 20 billion dollars, was invested abroad, half of it in the British empire. The French invested 8.7 billion dollars abroad, the Germans 6 billion. The German penetration of the Ottoman empire, centered around the Bagdad railroad and supported by German political and military diplomacy, was more typical of imperialism than was the rest of German colonial policy. Some of the small European countries like Switzerland, Belgium, and the Netherlands also made considerable foreign investments. Europe was the world's banker,† and inevitably the financiers exercised great pressure on their governments. It is an unanswerable problem

* Cf. Royal Institute of International Affairs: *Germany's Claim to Colonies*, Information Department Papers, No. 23 (London: 1938).
† Cf. H. Feis: *Europe, the World's Banker, 1870–1914* (New Haven; 1930). Compare also J. Viner: "International Finance and Balance of Power Diplomacy, 1880–1914," *Southwestern Political and Social Science Quarterly* (1929), Vol. IX; pp. 407–51, and E. Staley: *War and the Private Investor* (New York: 1935).

whether or not Europe would have fared better if there had been a smaller capital accumulation and a wider distribution of profits through higher wages in Europe. The migration of European capital created the conditions for an expansion of overseas production, which meant also an additional market for European industrial goods. The increased production of primary products like wheat, rice, copper, tin, and rubber helped to keep the teeming millions of Europe working. Industrial capitalism demanded a system of world-wide interchange.

Trade rivalries and colonial competition increased, but no wars between the European nations resulted directly from these tensions. All the colonial conflicts between Britain and Germany, Britain and France, Britain and Russia were somehow settled by diplomatic means. Some of them rankled. Probably the French had not forgotten Fashoda as late as 1940, and Anglo-Russian disagreements in the Middle East were only superficially patched up by the Anglo-Russian accord of 1907. Still, though nerves were frayed and remained sensitive, no war originated from these struggles. The financial and commercial interests at stake added to the acerbity of international relations, but financiers and businessmen remained conscious of the great losses they would suffer in war.

Economic and political forces were closely intertwined in the age of imperialism. Often investors dragged the governments into intervention on their own behalf, but on the other hand, many times the political authorities pushed them into action. Probably the most important example of the latter type of investment was the French loans to Russia; 2.25 billion dollars, about a quarter of all the foreign investments of France, went to Russia. But for the prodding of the French Government the French banks would not have granted these loans, since they constituted a dubious capitalistic venture in view of the financial insolvency of czarist Russia. The French funds were needed to bring about and to bolster the Franco-Russian alliance. A very substantial part of them was used, not for profitable economic projects, but for the improvement of Russian military power and mobility.

Modern industrial capitalism changed the social structure of the individual European states, but it did not basically transform the national motivations of international affairs. It altered, however, both the forms and the range of international relations.

We have already reviewed the changing forms of diplomacy in the age of imperialism; we must discuss one more development of importance, the militarization of the modern European states. The period between 1871 and 1914 has often been called the period of "armed peace." In a way any age of European history could be given this name, but the military element was at that time more conspicuous than in earlier ages. Modern industrial capitalism in an era of growing population and prosperity enabled the states to organize bigger navies and armies than ever before. In the eighteenth century, France was the first European power whose army was as big as the Roman army under Emperor Augustus. After 1815 every great continental state could boast of such an army. After 1850 and again after 1871 peacetime armies grew even larger. Modern industries could equip these armies with ever deadlier weapons. The frightful casualties of the Austro-Prussian and Franco-German wars showed how machines were multiplying man's destructive capacity. And the new mass forces and the increased fire power were made even more effective by modern communications.

Napoleon's generalship had already demonstrated what could be done by using bigger forces and increased mobility. The wars of the eighteenth century were wars of limited risks. Soldiers were few and consequently not easily expendable. The movement of armies was made difficult by poor roads and the scarcity of food. The strategy of the eighteenth century was one of maneuver and of gaining points of advantage, such as a single fortress or province. Not the absolute defeat but the maximum attrition of the enemy was the true military objective. This strategy char-

acteristic of the age of absolutism and mercantilism was
abandoned by Napoleon.

Napoleon aimed at the annihilation of the armed forces
of his enemies and achieved it at what he called "lightning"
speed and at great risk. He had at his disposal greater
manpower and financial resources than the absolute monarchs had commanded. Napoleon did not hesitate to use all
the resources of France and of any country that he conquered in order to gain absolute decisions on the battlefield and dictate peremptory political terms to the defeated. Military action, Napoleon demonstrated, could not
only conquer provinces and colonies but also destroy old
and great nations in a single morning of combat.

The fearful lesson was not forgotten, though it was
somewhat repressed after Napoleon's final defeat. Economic
exhaustion and political reaction combined to keep modern
militarism within bounds. Large armies had been built during the French Revolution.* Carnot's *levée en masse* had
introduced the revolutionary idea that the right of modern
national citizenship found its complement in the obligation
of all the citizens to lend their strength to the defense of
the nation. Napoleon had toned down the Jacobin principle
of universal national service very considerably by granting
special exemptions to the *bourgeoisie,* but the draft had allowed him to build up the big armies that he led to many
victories. The restored Bourbon monarchy naturally went
even further in granting special exemptions from military
service. As a result the French army remained a semi-
professional army till 1872. The average soldier of the
French army of 1870 was supposed to have served for
eight years.

Prussia adopted universal military service in the years of
liberation from Napoleon. The small and poor state could
hope to create a large army only through conscription. The
Prussian reformers expected that a citizens' army would

* See the author's article "Professional Army Versus Military
Training," *The Annals of the American Academy of Political and
Social Science* (1945), Vol. CCXLI, pp. 123 ff.

display a higher morale than the mercenaries of Prussian absolutism. Since they also hoped that the new military system would help create a civic spirit in Prussian citizens, they wanted the conscript to serve in the army and army reserve only for relatively few years. Thereafter he was to join a national guard that was to have its own officers and was to be linked to the organs of local self-government introduced after 1807.

The idea of liberalizing the Prussian state through the reorganization of the army failed, as did many other liberal reform plans of the years 1807–19. Once the political reaction established its hold over the government the national guard idea was not further developed. Finally, William I's war minister Roon presented in the early 1860's an army bill that made universal military service nothing but a convenient system of recruitment for the standing army and its war reserve. And Bismarck's policy assured to the *Junker* officer corps complete control over Prussia's armed forces, which were directly subject to the king.

It was this reorganized army, resting on national conscription but converted into an instrument of a homogeneous professional officer class, that won the wars of 1866 and 1870–1 under Moltke. Under the influence of the German victories all the continental European states introduced universal military service as the most effective system for the organization of mass armies, and it formed the common basis of the subsequent expansion of the European armies.

Moltke's strategy had created in the heart of the Continent a new and powerful empire, and this fact by itself provided other nations with an incentive to arm. But it had also laid bare the terrifying effects that military might could produce in the age of modern capitalism. As late as 1840 it would have taken many weeks to assemble the whole Prussian army at a given place, since it was spread from Aachen to Tilsit. In 1866 the Prussian army was fully deployed along the Bohemian frontier in two weeks, and Moltke had even withdrawn the Prussian troops from the Rhine, since he trusted that in case of need he could move the army from Bohemia to southern Germany fast enough to meet a French military intervention. The railroads and the many new highways made mobility as well as concentration of forces possible.

But even more disquieting was the new relationship of war and peace that came thereby into being. Since the speed of mobilization was of vital significance, plans of mobilization had to be drawn up long beforehand. Every member of a nation liable for military duty had to know his place in the war machinery before war broke out. Whereas Napoleon made his military decisions on the battlefield, the modern European generals planned their campaigns and battles in peacetime and called upon their governments to implement their plans not only by granting them the necessary numbers of troops but by building the necessary railroad lines for their timely deployment. Thus an ever growing part of the peacetime activities of governments was absorbed by war preparations.

It is not enough to conceive of the process of militarization as the enlarging of armies in relative proportion to the growing population and the resources of the European nations. The changes caused by the militarization of Europe were structural as well. Previously merchants or travellers could cross all political frontiers without special permits and passports except in Russia; but militarization laid the groundwork for treating the national societies as independent, isolated entities. In the contracting geographical conditions of the age of modern capitalism the national states, for reasons of defense, grew more like medieval cities. The walls, gates, and moats were not visible as yet, but their blueprints were under way. In retrospect we can easily discern the beginnings of social organization for total war. The military leaders of the age, being themselves children of the social order that industrial capitalism had produced, thought they possessed the answer to the dangers that war posed to modern civilization. They believed that the existing social conditions would be

strained to the breaking point by a long general war
among the great powers. But they were confident that the
modern war organization and strategy would make future
wars short armed conflicts, like Moltke's wars of 1866 and
1871.

But the keen apprehension felt about any change of the
balance of military forces resulted in the race of armaments and diplomatic alliances. The growth of army expenditure in the British empire between 1870 and 1890
was about 350 per cent, in France 250 per cent, in Russia 400 per cent, in Austria-Hungary almost 450 per cent,
in Italy almost 350 per cent, in Germany 1,000 per cent.
The strength of the highly industrialized states was reflected in the per capita cost of the military expenditure.
The individual Britisher contributed $3.74 in 1870, $4.03
in 1890, $8.53 in 1914, the German $1.33, $2.95, $8.52,
the Frenchman $3.03, $4.87, $7.33; the comparative figures
for Russia were $1.34, $1.32, $2.58, and for Italy, $1.44,
$2.63, $3.81.*

The size of the military establishment and the assumed
conditions of future warfare profoundly affected the conduct of diplomatic relations. The eighteenth century had
called war the *ultima ratio regum.* One may reject this
specious label, yet admit that the wars of the eighteenth
century, though often enough grossly materialistic, still
were to a much higher degree instruments of a rational
policy than are modern wars. The gigantic power amassed
in the military juggernauts and the dramatic speed required for their effective application hung like the sword
of Damocles over the heads of the statesmen of the pre-
World-War-I era. Their freedom of action was gravely
handicapped.

The closeness of the military and political situation of
Europe formed a strange contrast to the world-wide activities of her people. Many million European emigrants went
to the Americas and Australia. Most of them were poor

* Q. Wright: *A Study of War* (Chicago: 1942), Vol I, pp.
670 f.

but could be absorbed by and contribute to the rapidly rising wealth of their countries of adoption, since in the same period European investment capital helped in the expansion of the economy of these new worlds. Elsewhere, particularly in the colonial regions, European capital and with it European merchants, financiers, and engineers were busy developing the resources of the new world economy.

It is not necessary at this point to discuss the negative aspect of Europe's colonial policies, nor do we inquire into the question of whether or not Europe would have done better to spend through wages a large percentage of the high capitalistic profits that formed the bulk of the capital that she exported. Europe could possibly have achieved a more secure social structure in such circumstances. But at the beginning of the twentieth century not only did the capitalists of the leading European countries enjoy their riches, but the European laborer had a better diet. drank coffee and tea, and smoked tobacco, while the imports of raw materials from overseas kept the wheels of European industries turning and provided jobs.

In the creation of a world-wide economy of exchange, transportation was of fundamental importance. The modern iron steamship, which came into use in the 1870's, made maritime traffic safe, reliable, speedy, and cheap. Indian rice and tea, Argentine beef, American and Canadian grain could now compete on the European market and reach the European breakfast or dinner tables. But with this new overseas production and European consumption, the Continent became increasingly dependent on imports and on the capacity of the non-European countries for buying European industrial products. What would happen to Europe if she were ever to be cut off from her sources of raw materials for a protracted period of time? And, we may add, what would occur in the world at large if its close contact with Europe were to be disrupted?

The establishment of a world economy was not immediately followed by an all-inclusive system of world politics. The policies of the European powers ranged far and wide over the globe. But until 1917, or at least till the last years of the nineteenth century, two separate political systems existed, one in the New World, the other in the Old. Quite apart from the profitable economic ties that bound the two systems together, there were many political connections between them. Political tussles occurred, but the European nations in general respected the Monroe Doctrine, and the United States abstained from active participation in the diplomatic controversies of Europe.

Surprisingly, the events in the Far East between 1895 and 1905 produced a distinct trend toward the merger of the two political systems. The disintegration of the Chinese empire and the ensuing struggle of the European powers to protect their markets or to acquire possessions on the Asiatic mainland brought into being a new magnetic field of world politics to which both systems were attracted. Russia was strategically best placed to expand into China and actually pressed hardest for direct control. Here as elsewhere Britain was the strongest opponent of Russian expansion, but the forces at her disposal were not equal to the task. British foreign policy, therefore, welcomed the appearance of new powers in the Far East. The decision of the United States to retain the Philippines after the Spanish-American War of 1898 was applauded by Britain, for it added American weight to the attempt to keep the door of China open to Western trade. But this addition did not seem enough. More direct means were needed to stop Russian progress. They were found in the Empire of the Rising Sun.

Japan was the first and best example of a non-Western community that adapted itself quickly to the technological and industrial methods of the West. It was the United States that in 1854 had induced Japan to open herself to Western influence and the developments that within less than half a century made her a generally recognized great power. Britain saw in Japan a logical ally to fight Russian encroachments on China and concluded an alliance with her in 1902. This alliance was negotiated at a time when

Russo-Japanese tension, chiefly over Manchuria, had already reached a high pitch. Thus, it contributed to the outbreak of the Russo-Japanese war in 1904, in which Japan established her ascendancy in the Far East. The United States had become herself a Far Eastern power in 1898, but, as a nation, only in a half-hearted way. The annexation of the Philippines and Guam had little popular support in the United States. The American Government could not turn the open-door principle into a guarantee for the integrity of China and had to try to deflect Japan from the Philippines. Japanese rule of Korea, which an American fleet had opened to Western trade, seemed as unobjectionable from the American point of view as the exclusion of Russia from Manchuria.

The United States offered her good services for bringing about peace in the Far East, and at Portsmouth, New Hampshire, Japanese and Russian diplomats worked out a settlement of the first war between two great powers since 1871. In the eyes of the contemporaries it was the first war between a Western and non-Western great power. But in terms of world history the greatest significance of the events of 1905 was the first emergence of a system of world politics. Never before had European, American, and Asiatic policies interacted as they did in this fateful year. America was drawn into active political participation outside the Western hemisphere and European affairs, for the first time, felt the impact of the war immediately. France was deprived of the potential benefits of her Russian alliance, and the recent French entente with Britain, the ally of Japan, was in the circumstances a doubtful insurance. Germany used the opportunity for an attempt to break up the Anglo-French entente, or at least to show up its political weakness, by raising the Moroccan problem. Among other arguments Germany employed the open-door principle, thereby begging American support for her Moroccan policy.

It is not necessary to describe in detail these and other aspects of the international crisis of 1905. It was the first "global" crisis in the sense that the course of events in Europe, Asia, and America was determined by the political interaction of the three continents. A system of world powers seemed to absorb all continental or regional political systems.

The world received in 1905 a first glimpse of the future global age. But in the decade after 1905 world politics appeared to relapse into its old forms again. Though Asia remained in ferment, the United States cultivated its insular position in world affairs, and Europe concentrated on her own grave troubles. Considering its origins it is most questionable that the war that broke out in Europe in August 1914 was a *world* war. In its beginnings it was only a great European war. But the elements that were to transform this European catastrophe into a world-wide conflict were already present.

IV

WORLD WAR I

1. THE GREAT EUROPEAN WAR, 1914–17

THE formation of the Franco-Russian alliance
in the early 1890's seemed to have placed Britain in an
enviable position. While the Franco-Russian and German-
Austrian-Italian blocs kept each other at bay, Britain appeared free to attend to her imperial overseas interests.
But Britain's "splendid isolation" did not prove as comfortable a situation as British statesmen originally felt it
to be. Suspicious as the continental powers were of each
other, they were even more preoccupied with ideas of expansion beyond Europe. Russia gave preference to the attainment of her aims in the Far East. France was en-
grossed in her African schemes, and Germany was fishing
with meager results wherever the waters were troubled.

It was never likely that the three continental powers
could form the close continental alliance of which William
II often dreamed. The Franco-German enmity was at
times dormant but always remained a political reality of
the first order. The Balkan conflicts kept Austria-Hungary
and Russia apart. Since Germany as a rule supported the
Viennese policies and was now actively engaged in building
up interests of her own in the Turkish empire, Russo-
German relations, though not always hostile, were never
trusting. But vis-à-vis the British empire the political divisions of the European continent seemed to lose much of

their acuteness. The continental powers hardly ever acted in full concert, but in colonial matters they displayed a common anti-British attitude, and the sum total of the European agitation was quite formidable. The South African tribulations, culminating in the Boer War of 1898–1901, had served since 1896 as a clear warning against the dangers of complete isolation.

Around the turn of the century the British began earnestly to review their stakes in world affairs with the intention of giving up positions that did not seem vital or that were obviously indefensible. Probably by far the greatest achievement of British diplomacy in terms of world history was the establishment of close Anglo-American relations. Prudent concessions in the Venezuela question in 1899 and the recognition of American control of the projected Panama Canal in 1901 ushered in an era of growing Anglo-American friendship. The British statesmen wished to exclude war between the two nations forever. They also hoped that the United States would play an active role in the Pacific and the Far East and would co-operate with Britain in this region. The great significance that the Anglo-American understanding was to assume in Europe after 1914 was not foreseen.

The most imposing task of British foreign policy was the defense of the huge perimeter around the southern extensions of Russia. As late as 1879 this meant in the eyes of the British Government the holding of a line from Constantinople through Iran and Afghanistan to Peking. But in the subsequent three decades Britain redefined this general line in certain respects and revised the diplomatic means of her containment policy. We have already seen that the British did not feel that they could defend China unaided by other powers and in 1902 had concluded the alliance with Japan.

British policy with regard to the western anchor of the line also shifted. Disraeli had continued to throw British support behind the Turkish empire, even when such a policy ran contrary to the aspirations of the Christian Balkan nations for full freedom. At the Congress of Berlin in 1878 he had compelled the Russians to accept a small Bulgaria. Disraeli's strong pro-Turkish policy, however, no longer represented Britain as a whole. In his memorable Mid-Lothian campaign of 1876 Gladstone had hurled his thunder against the Turkish atrocities in Bulgaria and thereby questioned the whole basis of British policy in the Near East, which had rested thus far on the belief that the Turks were the natural allies of Britain and could be reformed to satisfy Western liberal standards.

The events in Bulgaria in the years after 1878 destroyed many of the British fears that independent Balkan states would be mere tools of Russia. The Slav movement in southeastern Europe was a movement of peasants led by an intelligentsia largely composed of peasant sons. This democratic nationalism clashed with the authoritarian policy of czarist Russia. The Russian generals and bureaucrats roused the ire of the Bulgarian people. In 1885 the Bulgarians annexed East Rumelia, which the Congress of Berlin had denied them, and this time Britain supported the Bulgarian move while Russia opposed it. Panslavism was shown to be a propagandistic rather than realistic concept of Russian foreign policy.

While British policy in the Balkans thus became more flexible, wider changes were affecting the evolution of a new British attitude toward the Turkish empire. Since the modern iron vessel in the 1870's had made the north and south Atlantic sea routes and the route to India safe and much-travelled highways, the British interest in the commerce with the Russian Black Sea ports had rapidly diminished. Russian grain had once been an important item of British trade, but now North American grain or Indian rice was easily available. As a consequence Britain considered the Turkish Straits less important than in former times. The acquisition of the majority of the shares in the Suez Canal Company in 1874, the annexation of Cyprus in 1878, and the occupation of Egypt in 1882 shifted British interests toward the area between the eastern Mediterra-

nean, the Red Sea, and the Persian Gulf. It was judged
that the non-Turkish Levantine and Arabic parts of the
Ottoman empire formed the region vital to the defense of
the British empire, since this region enclosed all the routes
to India. In 1895 Salisbury proposed the partition of the
Ottoman empire, which Germany opposed, having already
assumed the role of the protector of the "sick man" of
Europe. Britain did not object to the German policy in
Turkey except in so far as it might appear later on to in-
fringe on British plans in the Persian Gulf sphere. Britain
saw no reason to take any other exception to a German
policy that would chill German-Russian relations. In any
event, after 1895 there was no indication that Britain
again wanted any sentry duty against Russia at the Turkish Straits. Apparently Britain did not feel any qualms
when she promised Russia future control of the Straits in
1915.

Since Britain was now concentrating her interest upon
the eastern Mediterranean it was highly desirable that she
should be able to administer Egypt without inimical foreign intervention. Foreign domination of the Sudan—which
automatically meant the control of the upper reaches of
the Nile, the river on which the whole economy of
Egypt depended—would make easy such outside inter-
ference. This was what France tried to achieve, but when
she met stern British resistance at Fashoda in 1898 she re-
treated. It was also possible, however, to create in occupied Egypt difficulties from within. In all financial matters
the British needed either the French or the German vote
on the international boards that had been set up after
Egypt's declaration of bankruptcy in 1876. Germany took
advantage of the Anglo-French antagonism by embarrassing the British administration of Egypt and thus extract-
ing diplomatic concessions elsewhere. When Anglo-German
tension grew as the result of the naval race, to be discussed later, British foreign policy attempted to free itself from any dependence on Germany by the direct negotiation of the issues outstanding with its foremost colonial

rival, France. The Anglo-French entente of 1904 succeeded in composing the colonial differences between the two countries. The core of the treaty was the agreement on French support of British policy in Egypt in exchange for British support of French policy in Morocco.

In 1907 Britain also settled by peaceful compromise her main controversies with Russia over Tibet, Afghanistan, and Iran. It is very doubtful, in fact improbable, that Russia would have accepted this settlement if she had not been weakened by the Japanese war of 1904-05 and the subsequent revolution in Russia. Moreover, the war with Japan had put a stop to Russian expansion in the Far East and had made Russia anxious to resume her struggle for the Turkish Straits. The Anglo-Russian agreement of 1907 was considered to be a steppingstone to a future revision of the Straits regime. Both the Anglo-French entente and the Anglo-Russian agreement were on the surface nothing but settlements of non-European or colonial problems. Yet, though they were concluded to stabilize the existing colonial order, they were also intended to allow the three powers to check Germany.

The original decision of Britain to contract its world-wide positions and ease the burdens of empire by compromising the major colonial conflicts was not made with any specific reference to Germany. As a matter of fact, between 1898 and 1902, that is, after the big German naval bills of 1898 and 1900, some British statesmen would have liked an Anglo-German alliance. But the growing realization that German naval policy was a threat to British security became the most important single factor that induced the British to move closer to the Franco-Russian group and later on to treat the entente with France of 1904 and the agreement with Russia of 1907 more and more as virtual European alliances.

William II's love of naval affairs enabled Admiral Alfred von Tirpitz to build a big German navy. He persuaded the Emperor that a large cruiser fleet could not protect the German colonies and German overseas trade, but that a battle fleet, even if originally it was of inferior size, could bring Britain to her senses. Tirpitz actually hoped to achieve eventual naval parity with Britain, but he camouflaged his ultimate aims by the announcement of his "risk theory." According to this spurious set of ideas, Germany was to build a fleet big enough to destroy a substantial part of the strongest navy afloat, which after such losses would be outmatched by a smaller navy. Thus the risk of losing her naval supremacy would keep Britain from attacking a power in possession of a reasonably big navy.

The strategic and tactical thinking behind the German naval building program was in every respect unsound; the political consequences were outright disastrous.* It was an irrevocable fact of geography that the British Isles cut athwart all German overseas routes. Whereas other trading nations, like the United States and Japan, were at least masters of their own home waters, Britain, not Germany, inevitably ruled the North Sea. Mahan in 1902 described the situation very clearly. "The dilemma of Great Britain is that she cannot help commanding the approaches to Germany by the very means essential to her own existence as a state of the first order." † Obviously Britain was not going to surrender the keys to her islands and empire. In 1904 she began to concentrate the bulk of her naval forces in home waters. The alliance with Japan and the understanding with France were helpful in the strategic shift. Then Britain entered upon a building program designed to give her a safe margin of superiority over the German navy. Temporarily she was in grave danger of losing her superiority when she started the construction of the battleships of the Dreadnought type; for the British Admiralty wrongly assumed that German naval yards would not be capable of turning out Dreadnoughts for some years to come. But, since the new-type men o'war

---

* The best discussion of German naval strategy is H. Rosinski: "Strategy and Propaganda in German Naval Thought," in *Brassey's Naval Annual 1945* (New York: 1945), pp. 125–50.

† *Ibid.*, p. 130.

outclassed all the old ships, the naval race between the two countries started almost from zero, and by 1908 Britain had gained a relatively secure, though not too comfortable, lead.

The events of World War I demonstrated the fallacy of the risk theory. A secondary navy, as the German fleet was, in spite of its well-built vessels, fine armor, guns, and well trained crews, could never hope to wrest command of the sea from a superior navy. In order to gain command of the sea a strategic offensive is called for, which requires at the very minimum parity, but preferably superiority. Tirpitz and the German admirals completely overlooked the fact that the German navy was not even in a position to force upon the British the battle that in their opinion was the crucial test of the "risk theory." They assumed quite naïvely that the British would send their fleet into the North Sea to seal the estuaries of the German rivers. It never occurred to them that the British navy could simply close the entrances to the North Sea from Scapa Flow and thereafter inflict as much damage on the German fleet and accept as much punishment from it as was compatible with the continued exercise of the command of the sea. That the British could do so was shown in the battle of Jutland of May 31, 1916. The losses of the British Grand Fleet were much heavier than those of the German navy, but the German fleet was in full retreat when Admiral Jellicoe broke off the battle in order to preserve the superiority of the British navy over any possible rival, which in his opinion included even the navy of the United States.

Other ideas of Tirpitz proved equally fatuous. He showed an abysmal lack of understanding of the economic strength of Britain as well as of the practical sense and patriotism of her citizens when he expressed the belief that the financial strain imposed upon Britain by the naval race would eventually make her ready to compromise. Nevertheless, the German naval challenge imposed very serious pressures upon British politics. Britain's freedom of

political action was limited. She was constrained to keep
other naval powers on her side and, naturally, to isolate
Germany as much as possible. The Germans, with their
congenital inclination to see the mote in their opponents'
eyes and unwillingness to discover the beam in their own,
called this a policy of encirclement; yet Bismarck's policy
toward France had been precisely the same. Sir Edward
Grey no more planned to choke Germany than the Iron
Chancellor had intended to destroy France. Grey's hope
was that once he had gained diplomatic preponderance for
Britain he could try for a *détente* between the two European camps, or, even better, for the restoration of a European concert—a goal he came actually close to achieving
at the time of the Balkan Wars of 1912–13, when the
European ambassadors' conferences in London helped to
avoid a general conflagration. No serious student of history has ever questioned Grey's personal intentions, but
doubts have been raised about his political determination
and diplomatic skill. He feared lest his approaches to
Germany be misunderstood by Russia and France. Consequently, he moved cautiously, maybe overcautiously, but
this discretion was fully understandable considering the
negative attitude that Germany displayed on most occa-
sions.

Tirpitz's naval building program was the greatest single
factor that forced Britain into close co-operation with the
Continent. As a matter of fact, except for brief moments
Britain had never in her history been so closely and irrevocably integrated in the European political system as in
the decade before the outbreak of World War I. Germany's naval policy was suicidal. If Germany wanted to
break the natural stranglehold that Britain held on her
maritime communications, there was only one way—to build
a navy at least as big and preferably bigger than the British fleet. Moreover, Germany should have secured her rear
by a close understanding with Russia and have concluded
as many alliances as possible all over the world in order
to compel Britain to spread her forces far over the globe.

Presumably, the German monarchy could have reached an understanding with czarist Russia, though the price might have been high after 1894. In all likelihood it would have included not only the abandonment of an active German policy in Turkey but also some arrangement for the future of the Habsburg empire.

It is highly speculative to raise these issues, and nobody can pronounce on them with full certainty. In any event, it can be said that a serious rather than foolhardy German attempt to overthrow Britain's naval supremacy would have required the subordination of all the activities of German foreign policy to this one single objective. Short of this, Germany would have been better advised if she had directed her energies exclusively to continental ends. But the leaders of the German government, William II, Chancellor Bülow, and Tirpitz, never faced up to the necessity of a logical and consistent foreign policy. In Germany semi-absolutist government was usually defended by arguments that were originally advanced by Bismarck. This regime was supposed to produce a well reasoned, unified, and steady policy beyond the reach of party prejudices and party fluctuations, a policy needed by a country located in the center of Europe and surrounded by many dangers. But actually William II's ideas were forever vacillating, and the various agencies of the German government, the foreign office, the navy department, and the army, conducted contradictory foreign policies. Each of these policies, though in varying degrees, rested on flimsy premises, since none of them took into consideration the over-all potentialities of German foreign policy.

In contrast Britain, which was so often accused of changing her foreign policies according to shifting parliamentary majorities, developed a continuity of foreign policy in spite of the growing democratization of British political life. When Sir Edward Grey and the liberal party took over the government in 1905–06, they accepted the reorientation of British foreign policy that Lord Lansdowne had inaugurated by the Anglo-Japanese alliance and the

Anglo-French entente. The British people supported this continuity of policy. If there was criticism, it was not so much of the general direction of British foreign policy as of its constitutional procedure. Once the secret articles of the Anglo-French entente became known in 1911, a lively discussion arose over the desirability of making parliamentary or democratic control of the conduct of international relations more effective. This discussion issued in a demand for abolishing secret diplomacy and replacing it by "open" diplomacy, a new ideal that struck a sympathetic chord in American hearts and made a great impression on Woodrow Wilson.*

Outside of the Social Democratic party, which by 1912 was receiving 35 per cent of the German vote, the foreign policies of the imperial government were almost universally supported by the German people. The popularity of the various measures differed, however, among the various classes of the population. The *Junkers,* who were congenital army people and also agrarians, were not particularly enamored with William II's naval policy. A typical Prussian *Junker* looked down on the British money-changers and traders but preferred to do so from a distance. He could not, of course, openly revolt against the emperor. It is interesting to note that Germany's renowned chief-of-staff of the army, Count Schlieffen, never raised his voice against the diversion of military funds to the navy, though in all his thinking about the defense of Germany the navy had no place. The turn from Bismarck's "continental" politics to "world" politics had its most enthusiastic supporters and promoters among the German *bourgeoisie.* The large and prosperous German middle classes from the big industrialist to the storekeeper and from the high bureaucrat to the university professor and school teacher were

---

* A House of Commons Debate on parliamentary control of foreign policy took place on November 17, 1911. In 1912 the British Government presented these papers: *Treatment of International Questions by Parliaments in European Countries, the United States, and Japan,* Cd. 6102 (*Miscellaneous* No. 5, 1912).

the chief believers in this new version of German *Realpolitik*, so completely bare of the realism of Bismarck, whom they worshipped, and so empty of European *Kultur*, of which the German middle classes claimed to be the true guardians.

The German political and social system did not produce a sense of political and, least of all, European responsibility. Tirpitz exploited the political gullibility of the German middle classes and their craving for national grandeur to the full. He was not only the technical architect of the ill-fated German navy but also the first nationalistic manipulator of mass opinion in Germany. His ability to organize mass support had something of the Hitlerian touch, although the Admiral addressed a higher social class than did Corporal Hitler. During World War I, Tirpitz built up the popular organization known as the "fatherland party," which supported the expansionist policies of the German general staff. His last significant intervention in German politics took place in 1925, when his efforts made Hindenburg the candidate of the rightist parties in the presidential elections.

By forcing Britain to take sides in the alignment of the European powers, German naval policy completed the division of Europe into two political camps armed to the teeth and ready to take up open hostilities; for any misunderstanding could seriously affect the precarious balance of power on which the European nations had staked their security. The great powers succeeded in isolating the wars among the Balkan states because these states were small, but they found it impossible to localize a conflict in which a great power was involved. The Austro-Serbian crisis set off by the assassination of the heir to the Habsburg crown, Archduke Francis Ferdinand, on June 28, 1914, was used by the ruling groups of the empire to suppress once and for all the agitation for Yugoslav unity. They wished to humiliate Serbia, the state that could become the active leader, the Slav Piedmont, of the national movement. The Austrian and Magyar statesmen were fully aware that their policy could bring on war with Russia, but they argued that an Austro-Russian war was bound to occur sooner or later and was not an absolute danger for the Habsburg empire as long as German support was certain.

It was a policy of despair, not without a note of cynicism, that the Austro-Hungarian Government followed in July 1914. Europe had managed to live for a century without a general war, but the impact of nationalism on the least developed region of Europe and the desperate opposition of the older forces in that area produced the conflagration that enveloped the whole of Europe and eventually most of the world. For Germany, afraid of losing her last ally, backed Austria-Hungary to the hilt; France dreaded to be separated from Russia; Britain was apprehensive of alienating her French and Russian partners if she followed too independent a course of policy. Even so, the British Government tended rather to overrate its freedom of action in 1914. Some members of the British cabinet saw this weakness beforehand, but only the German invasion of Belgium made it clear to the majority of the cabinet and the British people. The German invasion gave Britain a lofty moral principle to defend, the sanctity of treaties and the rule of law. The restoration of the Lowlands had been one of the cornerstones of the European settlement of 1815, and after the Belgian revolution of 1830, the great powers again had found in concert a peaceful solution. But with the violation of the Belgian neutrality the last vital prop of the nineteenth century order of Europe was knocked down. The diplomatic balance of power had turned into a balance of military power.

The balance of power is a crude and often fallacious principle. Nobody can ever be absolutely certain that a given state enjoys superiority over, or even equality of power with, another state, and the comparative appraisal of groups of allied powers has to cope with an even larger number of unpredictable elements. The iron test of the balance of power lies in the very thing it is designed to stave off—war. And war appallingly often proves the weakness of all political calculation. The great European war of 1914–17 did so.

Each of the two camps, the Triple Entente and the Central Powers, was confident that it could not only balance but also outbalance the other. France, Britain, and Russia believed that they could overwhelm Germany and Austria-Hungary, if not in the early beginning, then certainly as soon as Russia could throw her millions into the fray and the British blockade began to tell. Germany on her part had planned to use the time gained by the slow military mobilization of Russia to concentrate her might in the West and defeat the French army; thereafter she had intended to turn eastward to stem the Russian tide. But the bold planning of the Prussian general staff was of no avail.

The project drafted by the chief-of-staff, Count Schlieffen, in 1905, better known as the Schlieffen plan, envisaged the annihilation of the French army by a wheeling movement of an all-powerful German right wing through Luxemburg, Belgium, and northern France. The plan was conceived at a time when Russia was unable to intervene in central Europe as a result of the Russo-Japanese War and internal unrest. The prevalent German sentiment has been that the master plan of victory that Schlieffen had bequeathed to his successor was emasculated and poorly executed by the younger Moltke. These accusations are not unfounded, but it should not be forgotten that by 1914 the Russian army was capable of participating in the initial phase of the war by dispatching strong advance forces and that the British had built up a small but not insignificant expeditionary corps. Although the French had to bear the brunt of the German attack, the Russian penetration into East Prussia and the presence of British troops at the western front were important elements in frustrating the German conquest of France.

The German offensive was fought to a standstill at the Marne in early September, 1914, and thereafter no strategic success was achieved at the western front for almost four years, in spite of the unprecedented slaughter of millions of Europe's finest youth and manhood. Nobody can say how much budding genius and talent of Europe was interred in the mass graves of France between 1914 and 1918. It is certain, however, that there was much less genius and talent in Europe after World War I than before.

The German plans were disappointed both in the east and west. Whereas in the west the Germans failed to reach their objectives, they overshot their mark in the east. The small covering forces left by Germany in the east, which were designed to fall back behind the Vistula, defeated the Russian armies that had broken into East Prussia. The generalship of Hindenburg and his chief-of-staff Ludendorff, who provided the plans for this military victory, seemed to stand out as shining examples of great military leadership. Under their influence German offensive operations were shifted to a large extent to the East. By 1917 these efforts had yielded decisive results, but this success was to backfire.

The March Revolution of 1917 in Russia liberalized the Russian government and at the same time attempted to rally the Russian army and people for a supreme effort. The Kerenski government was soon swept away by the Bolshevist October Revolution, which promised the conclusion of peace to the Russian people. To Lenin this promise meant peace at practically any price, since he was convinced that the coming world revolution would turn all the existing international agreements into scraps of paper. Thus in the early months of 1918 Germany was able to impose the two treaties of Brest-Litovsk on the Soviet Union and the Ukraine. Russia was deprived of all the European possessions that she had acquired in the course of two centuries and was further weakened by the creation of a separate Ukrainian state. In addition, the treaties contained provisions that gave Germany a stranglehold over the economic life of Russia. Similar provisions were included in the Rumanian peace treaty, which was concluded in May, 1918.

Unfortunately for the Germans their demands were so sweeping that large numbers of German troops were needed to occupy the eastern states, which were threatened by internal revolution. Ludendorff's political passion now began greatly to interfere with his military plans. He wanted to bring on a decision in the West before the Americans could intervene in great numbers, but this move called for the concentration of all available German forces in the West. For the first time since 1914 the Germans enjoyed superior strength in France when they launched their offensive in March, 1918. But largely due to Ludendorff's political adventures in the East their margin of superiority was very small and, as events confirmed, much too small for large-scale offensive operations. With the loss of the offensive it was only a question of time when the Allies, now continuously reinforced by American troops, would roll the German armies back to the Rhine.

It is true, however, that the European Allies of 1914 did not defeat the Central Powers by their own strength. Only the entrance of the United States made the Allied victory possible. There was no European balance of power. Events at the eastern front prevented Britain and France from taking full advantage of their alliance with Russia. The land of the czars had millions of soldiers but not the industries to arm them nor adequate transportation to move huge armies and their supplies. If Churchill's scheme to seize the Turkish Straits in 1915 had been successful, western supplies could have been shipped to Russia and the West-East alliance could have been activated in many respects. As long as Germany, however, was sitting athwart the lines of communication between Russia and western Europe, she could select the place of her attack. In her strategic isolation Russia succumbed to the German onslaught.

After the great disappointments resulting from the fighting in the early months of the war, the Allies began to look around for new allies who might help them to tip the balance against Germany and Austria-Hungary. They

brought—or one could almost say bought—Italy and Rumania into the war in 1915 and 1916. Dire military necessity seemed to make the price paid in the form of political
promises inevitable. Thus in the secret treaties with the
two states the Allies sacrificed liberal ideals on the altar of
Mars and nationalism. Other secret treaties were concluded
among the original allies, the first of them again necessitated by military circumstances. The British attempt to
force the Turkish Straits in 1915 made it desirable to as-
sure Russia that the Gallipoli expedition was not a design
to establish western European domination over Turkey, but
was undertaken in order to strengthen the inter-Allied position in the war against the Central Powers. Consequently,
Russia received a pledge that within certain limitations she
could control Constantinople after the war. Additional
agreements, the Franco-Russian agreement of 1916, for instance, under which the two powers promised to support
each other in annexing the Rhineland and East Prussia re-
spectively, were not directly the outcome of military needs,
unless one is inclined to interpret the mutual grants of
future national gains as morale boosters.

In any event, the secret treaties did not bring victory
to the European Allies. Nevertheless, Italy's and Rumania's
entrance delayed the German timetable of operations. The
opening of the Italian front proved an additional strain
on the Austro-Hungarian army that had been badly mauled
by the Russians and Serbians in the early months of the
war. The Germans had to reinforce all the theaters of
operations. Thus precious time was gained for Britain
to mobilize her manpower for active intervention in the
war. For the first time in modern history Britain was
forced to build up a huge citizens' army through universal
conscription. All the British wars of the earlier centuries
on the Continent were fought with small hired armies supported by armies of continental allies, which very often
were maintained by British subsidies. Now for the first
time Britain had to adopt the continental system of war
mobilization. It was fortunate for Britain that she decided

on a modest expansion of her army before 1914. In 1913 Britain spent one fifth of her defense expenditures on the army, whereas the Germans spent one fifth of their defense funds on the navy and four fifths on the army. But, whereas the German battlefleet, because of British naval strength, proved of little consequence in World War I, the small British army played a minor if important role even in the Marne battle of 1914 and served thereafter as the nucleus for the British wartime army, which by 1918 was probably stronger than the French army.

Still, not even the unprecedented military mobilization of British manpower created an Allied ascendancy over Germany. After the German defeat of Russia the European Allies could not have hoped any longer to turn the tables on Germany by their own efforts. They needed the help of the United States to force a decision.

2.   WORLD WAR AND WORLD SETTLEMENT, 1917–19

THE breakdown of the European balance of power during the war years of 1914–17 could not fail to affect the whole world. For Europe was the undisputed political, industrial, and financial center of the earth, and the European nations were locked in an internecine struggle, employing recklessly their rich resources for mutual destruction. What the absence of the European states from other global scenes meant could be learned at once by the new Japanese drive for expansion in the Pacific. The European war also shifted the foundations of American security.

The American Republic had gained its original independence as a result of the division between the two major colonial powers of eighteenth century Europe—Britain and France. The freedom of action enjoyed by the United States in the affairs of the Western hemisphere all through the nineteenth century had rested to a large extent on the rivalries among the European nations, which had kept them from large-scale political intervention in the New World.

But even more important was the fact that Britain controlled the oceans after 1815 and therefore was able to
block the continental European states in any attempted in-
terference with the political fortunes of the New World.
American foreign relations through the century prior to
1914 had been chiefly relations with Britain, and events had
shown that they could be maintained on a friendly
and peaceful level.

But the European war of 1914 threatened to destroy the
political system that had made possible America's relative
aloofness from world politics during the nineteenth century.
If the European Allies had been defeated, the United States
would have had to face on the eastern shores of the Atlantic a continent practically united under German leadership. The German alliance with the Turkish empire would
have extended Germany's sway to the eastern Mediterranean
and the Persian Gulf, and the defeat of Russia would have
enabled Germany to draw on the resources of Eurasia. This
huge accumulation of power would have been in the hands
of a state that in the war-time quarrels over the international law of the seas gave the United States a foretaste
of its dictatorial manners. The United States had good reason for associating herself with the Allies at a time when,
owing to the impending collapse of Russia, their cause was
in acute jeopardy. The American people were hardly aware
of these cogent reasons for the entrance of the United
States into the war and viewed American participation in it
entirely in the light of a crusade for freedom and democracy.

It is even doubtful whether Wilson and his advisers were
quite conscious of the pressure of fateful historical circumstances that forced the United States to support the Allies.
It was true that the American policy of neutrality toward
the European war was from the beginning strongly slanted
in favor of Britain, but this policy was never set forth in
terms of the American national interest; it was defended
by legal theories concerning the maritime rights of neu-
trals. If the Germans had paid more heed to these Ameri-

can declarations, war between the United States and Germany might have been avoided.*

But after 1916 Wilson defined additional aims of United States foreign policy. He declared that no future peace settlement could last unless the United States would participate in its guarantee, and he proposed a league of free nations to maintain world peace. This Wilsonian policy was eminently sound, but when enunciated in 1916 and January, 1917, it neglected the most immediate problem of whether or not the free nations needed American military help. The European war caused consternation and apprehension in the United States, but it was not fully understood as a vital threat to the historic foundations of her national security. It would have been better if President Wilson had reminded the American people of their own direct interest in the outcome of the European war. Many Americans conceived of America's participation in World War I as an exclusively idealistic venture, and after the fighting was over many concluded that American foreign policy under Wilson's leadership had attended to esoteric ends rather than to genuine American needs. The postwar revulsion of the American people towards the League and the Paris Peace treaties as well as the strength of American isolationism in the interwar period were partly prepared by the weakness in the formulation of the political motives of American action during World War I.

The United States entered the war in April, 1917, at a time when the European Allies were in mortal danger. The immediate contribution that America could make to the war was not negligible, though it was limited in scope. The American navy was ready for action and decisively assisted the British navy in checking the depredations of the German submarine. American financial and economic support also eased at once some of the problems of Allied war mobilization. But the state of American armaments did

* Cf. W. Lippmann: *U.S. Foreign Policy: Shield of the Republic* (Boston: 1943), pp. 33 ff; E. H. Buehrig: "Wilson's Neutrality Reexamined," *World Politics* (1950), Vol. III, pp. 1–19.

not permit any American intervention in the land warfare for another year to come, just when the European Allies had to bear the brunt of the fighting against the superior forces of the Central Powers.

The United States only "associated" herself with the Allies, thus reserving her freedom of action toward a future peace settlement. Wilson learned about the secret treaties soon after America's entry into the war, but he refused to take official notice of them. He felt that he could not express his opposition to the war aims contained in the secret treaties at a time when the war was in its most threatening stage and the United States was not yet fully engaged in the active battle. If, for example, the United States had openly expressed her disapproval of the secret Treaty of London in the spring or summer of 1917, Italian morale, which was sagging, might have been broken and irreparable damage been done to the cause of the powers fighting the Central Powers. Wilson recognized that only to the extent to which the United States assumed a substantial share of the actual fighting could she begin to press the universal acceptance of her own peace objectives. The President also hoped that the exhaustion of Europe would make the United States the natural guide in the postwar rehabilitation of the world.

The Bolshevist Revolution of November 1917, the ensuing Communist peace propaganda, which included the publication of the secret treaties, and the Peace Conference of Brest-Litowsk, which the United States and the Allies did not wish to see transformed into a general peace conference, compelled the heads of the Western governments to present to the world a concrete sketch of their war and peace aims. These aims were intended to rally the Western peoples for the supreme military test ahead of them and at the same time to serve as a program that would induce national or political groups in the enemy countries to oppose the war policies of their governments. In addition, the program had to be a general blueprint of a future world order.

The "trade-union" speech of Lloyd George on January 5
and Wilson's Fourteen Points address on January 8, 1918
sought to formulate such a program.

On this occasion Lloyd George came closer than ever
before to Wilson's liberalism. As a matter of fact, the aims
propagated by Lloyd George were hardly distinguishable
from those proclaimed by Woodrow Wilson, except, of
course, with regard to the freedom of the seas. If Lloyd
George paid less attention to the League than Wilson, it
was not due to any fundamental disagreement, but rather to
the fact that the British Government was still studying the
practical implications of the project that it had accepted in
principle. But then and later on Lloyd George failed to re-
nounce the secret treaties, and much of his personal idealism was compromised by his opportunistic political tactics.
In January, 1918, he wished to capture the enthusiasm of
the masses; months later he wanted to gain a parliamentary
majority at almost any price. He was a liberal at heart,
but also a demagogue, unwilling ever, even temporarily, to
lose popular favor.

Wilson's Fourteen Points speech and his subsequent
speeches on foreign affairs in 1918 became the great sign-
posts of a liberal world order. In contrast to the dissi-
pated "psychological" warfare of the Allies in World War
II, Allied political warfare in 1918 proved extremely effective, for it was based on a political program that both
attracted whole nationalities to the Allied side—some of
the component popular groups of the Habsburg empire, for
instance—and also held out to the defeated foe hope for
an ordered international and decent national life. When in
the summer of 1918 Germany and Austria-Hungary had to
recognize that they could not hope to win the war, when
the western front showed signs of breaking and the southeastern front in Turkey and Bulgaria collapsed, even Ludendorff, who had always felt nothing but scorn for the
Fourteen Points, saw in them the sheet anchor of a Germany in defeat. The German wartime dictator insisted that

Germany should have a parliamentary government and should request an armistice and peace on the basis of the Fourteen Points.

It was the German request for such an armistice, sent to Washington on October 5, that enabled Wilson to bring the question of Allied peace aims to a showdown. The Fourteen Points were not a program to which the European Allies, Britain, France, and Italy, were officially committed. While Wilson tried to exact from Germany further promises of internal democratization and thereby helped to precipitate the outbreak of the German revolution, the struggle for a uniform peace program went on among the Allies in Paris. Britain, France, and Italy were unwilling to commit themselves to the Fourteen Points, and only Colonel House's open warning at the supreme war council in Paris that under such circumstances the United States would proceed to conclude a separate armistice with Germany led to Allied agreement. Point Two, covering the American demand for freedom of the seas, was practically excluded, but the question of reparations, which the Fourteen Points had only sketchily dealt with, was formulated in clear terms, though the British, French, and others boldly challenged the meaning of the text at the peace conference.*

By an American note of November 5, 1918, signed by Secretary Lansing, Germany was duly informed of the Allied understanding and, if she accepted the political conditions, invited to dispatch a delegate to Compiègne to receive the military armistice conditions. This military armistice was exclusively French and British in origin. General Pershing advised against granting the Germans an armistice; he wanted the Allied armies to march to Berlin. Foch, considering the grievous losses that the Allies had suffered in four years of cruel fighting, was willing to accept an armistice, provided it secured the military and political objectives of the war. In his opinion, which was shared by other Allied generals, the Allied armies could not reach the Rhine before March,

* Cf. P. M. Burnett: *Reparation at the Peace Conference* (New York: 1940), with an introduction by I. F. Dulles.

1919. But if the Germans withdrew behind the Rhine and
agreed to hand over a substantial amount of their arms, the
Allies would achieve their military objectives without another dreadful winter of fighting and could also impose their
political terms, since Germany would be unable to resume
the battle. Foch himself considered the control of the
Rhineland the supreme war aim of France and tried to secure it through the military armistice that he proposed to
the heads of the Allied governments and dictated to the
Germans. The British added to the armistice the naval
chapters, which practically realized their foremost war aim,
namely the destruction of the German navy. When the
Germans signed the armistice on November 11th, they surrendered their capacity for resistance by military means to
the future political demands of the victors. Nevertheless, the armistice was no unconditional surrender. The
victor nations, bound among themselves to the Wilsonian
peace program by their Paris agreement, were under an
obligation to the defeated nations to construct a liberal
peace.

Just prior to the breakdown of Germany's military might
the Habsburg empire collapsed. But, whereas Germany, in
spite of the occupation and amputation of some of her
provinces, continued to be a big state, the Habsburg empire
dissolved into a number of states. The demise of the historic empire was the result of the revolt of its various
nationalities, of which some, the Yugoslavs, Rumanians, and
Poles, wanted to be united with groups or states outside
the boundaries of the former empire. Only Czechoslovakia
and, of course, Austria and Hungary themselves were "suc-
cession states" in the strict sense.

The revival of the nationalities of eastern Europe had
begun in the early nineteenth century largely under the influence of the German romanticism that had started with
Herder. But when the movement was transformed from one
of cultural regeneration into one of political liberation the
ideas of the French Revolution and with them the desire for
direct political co-operation with the West became more

dominant. There were, however, also those who expected
their national liberation from Russia. The Serbs, linked to
Russia by the same religious faith and similar monarchical
institutions, were most hopeful of Russian help: The Croats,
Slovenes, and the Czechoslovaks welcomed the Russian alliance with the western European powers as a guarantee of
victory over the Germans and Magyars, but they wanted to
live between the East and West; certainly they did not
want to rely exclusively or even predominantly on Russia.
The Poles, on the other hand, had hardly any good feelings
towards Russia. On the contrary, there were even Poles who
felt, after the German victories over Russia, that the creation of a Polish state could be solved in collaboration with
Germany; but the German treatment of Poland during
World War I and the absolute unwillingness of Germany
to consider the status of the Polish provinces of Prussia
frustrated any constructive attempt at German-Polish co-operation during World War I. On the whole it could be said
that Panslavism was chiefly a sentiment expressing common
Slav hostility against Germany; it was not a positive element
of unity among the Slavs, and least of all was it an incentive to accepting Russian hegemony.

The defeat of Russia by Germany and the rise of bolshevism orientated all the eastern European nations toward
the West, but without turning them into easy followers of
the western European powers. Each of them doggedly pur-
sued the goal of its own national independence, disregarding their mutual relations and also the long-range problems
of European community life. As soon as the three big powers that had ruled central and eastern Europe for the last
centuries collapsed, Czechoslovakia and Poland began to
feud; so did Rumania and Poland, and all of them displayed
vengeful enmity toward Austria and Hungary, which, incidentally, were themselves at odds once the Habsburg monarchy fell.

Britain and France had favored the dissolution of the
Habsburg empire early in the war. The Treaty of London
of May, 1915, with its lavish promises of Italian gains at

the expense of Austria-Hungary, showed that the Allies felt little concern about the future of the Habsburg empire, and in January, 1917, replying to President Wilson's inquiry into the war aims of the belligerents, the Allies publicly stated their support of the Slav and Rumanian national movements. Sympathy with the struggle of the nationalities in the Habsburg empire had originally been aroused at the time of the conclusion of the Anglo-French and Anglo-Russian ententes by a small group of French and English scholars like Louis Eisenmann, R. W. Seton-Watson, and Wickham Steed.* During World War I these men exercised great influence on both sides of the Atlantic through a periodical with the significant title *The New Europe*.†

The entrance of the United States into the war put temporary brakes upon the drive for full independence of the southeastern nationalities. American diplomacy hoped to reach a separate peace with Austria-Hungary. Even the Fourteen Points speech of January 8, 1918, proclaimed America's desire to see Austria-Hungary's place among the nations "safeguarded and assured," though her people "should be accorded the freest opportunity of autonomous development." But the failure of the secret peace negotiations with the Government of Emperor Charles of Austria-Hungary induced the United States to throw her full weight behind the disruptive national forces. The curious *de jure* recognition of the Czechoslovak committee of Masaryk and Beneš, which was not even a *de facto* government of Bohemia and Moravia, was the final seal of this policy. The military collapse of Germany and Austria-Hungary led to the dissolution of the Habsburg empire and the rise of the new states all along the eastern fringe of Europe from Finland to Yugoslavia. When the Paris Peace Conference con-

* L. Eisenmann: *Le compromis austro-hongrois de 1867* (Paris: 1904); R. W. Seton-Watson: *The Southern Slav Question* (London: 1911); H. Wickham Steed: *The Hapsburg Monarchy* (London: 1913).

† Harold Nicolson testifies to its great influence in his *Peacemaking 1919* (New York: 1939), p. 33.

vened in January, 1919, the political map of Europe had already been radically changed.

The year 1919 was the high watermark of democracy in
world history. Not even 1945 can be compared to that
year, since in 1945 the democratic nations shared their victory with the Soviet Union and the major spoils of victory went to the latter. In 1919 no autocratic or authoritarian power could obstruct the peace settlement, and peacemaking was the exclusive responsibility of the democratic
nations. Still, "the war to make the world safe for
democracy," a phrase first coined by H. G. Wells in
August, 1914 to describe the meaning of World War I,
brought forth before long the age of the dictators, and "the
war to end war" turned out to be the harbinger of even
greater disaster.

If we compare the Paris settlement of 1919 to the
Vienna settlement of 1815, it is obvious that some of the
fundamental elements that made for unity and mutual understanding among the peacemakers of Vienna were lacking
in 1919. The wars of 1812-15 had a clear common aim, the
defeat of Napoleon's revolutionary attempt at uniting the
Continent under his dictatorial power and the restoration
of the old European state system. The war of 1914–18 did
not have such a single common goal. Of course, the
immediate objective of the war, the destruction of Germany's overweaning power, was accepted as a general Allied
war aim, but no clarity existed among the victorious powers
about the type of Europe that they wanted to build or
rebuild, supposing, indeed, that they could construct a
European political system at all.

World War I had shown that the balance of Europe did
not exist any longer; in order to subdue the Central Powers
the intervention of the United States and also of the British
dominions was required. The United States played a
leading, and the British dominions a significant, role in the
making of the peace settlement of Paris in 1919. It was
natural that they wished to create a world settlement and
that they were little concerned about the resurrection of

the broken-down European system. The British Government, owing to its own world-wide commitments, easily fell in with this trend. In contrast, Clemenceau, more than any other Allied statesman, thought in terms of the restoration of a European balance of power and made a supreme effort to gain a peace that would place France in an unassailable position of military superiority over Germany. He therefore aimed at the amputation of a maximum of German territories, the blocking of the merger of Austria and Germany, the imposition of heavy reparations, and French control of the left bank of the Rhine.

To the rigid military mind of General Foch this program was the logical expression of French national interest; but Clemenceau himself was too wise to look at politics in such simple logical terms. The last great Jacobin knew the dynamic force of nationalism and realized that a treaty of this description would breed fiery German resentment. It was doubtful, furthermore, whether France by herself could make such a peace settlement effective. France would have succumbed to Germany in the war if it had not been for her Allies, and she had suffered grievous losses that not even victory could recover. Clemenceau was under no illusion that the future security of France did not depend principally on continued co-operation with Britian and the United States.

Although Clemenceau bargained hard to gain the French points, he compromised with Wilson and Lloyd George on the Rhineland issue. France received no German territory outside of Alsace-Lorraine. The Saar district was separated from Germany and France given a preponderant position in its administration, but it was to be under League auspices and a plebiscite was to take place after fifteen years to settle the final status of the region according to the wishes of its inhabitants. No separate Rhenish state was created, and though the Rhineland was demilitarized, its occupation by Allied troops was limited to fifteen years. In exchange for these stipulations made possible by Clemenceau's concessions, France was promised that if during the next fifteen years the Germans were to challenge the arrangements concerning the Rhineland, the United States and Britain would give her military assistance.

The most crucial of all the political problems of Europe was thus settled by arrangements that envisaged the continued participation of a non-European power in the maintenance of the European peace. In the Rhineland this co-operation took the form of a specific guarantee by individual nations. In general the universal League of Nations, composed of members from all continents, was supposed to safeguard the peace of Europe as a part of world peace. No conscious attempt was made to reconstruct a politically self-sufficient European system. Nobody could contend that a Europe similar to that of the nineteenth century could have been revived by the Paris Peace Conference, and the conference dealt almost exclusively with the claims of nations on the one hand and with the building of a world system on the other. The common problems concerned with Europe as a whole found no discussion.

No other political document could have offered as much guidance for the establishment of a peaceful international society as did the American constitution, and it was the greatness of Woodrow Wilson that he projected the American political tradition ably and eloquently into a liberal international faith. The weakness of Wilson's international program lay in the generality of many of its tenets and in the contradictory nature of some of them. The principle of national self-determination, for example, was not universally practicable, and in certain cases it conflicted with other Wilsonian principles, such as the demand of access to the seas for landlocked states. The generality of the Fourteen Points and their lack of absolute logical unity offered the opportunity for perverting Wilson's program at the peace conference by writing many nationalistic war gains into the final settlement. But with more good will Wilson's program could have been adapted to the historic conditions of the hour.

More serious was Wilson's ingrained belief that his abstract ideals could blot out certain realities of political life.

Walter Lippmann once pointed out that the Wilsonian principles were formulated on the basis of America's aloofness from world politics as it had existed due to specific and fortunate historical circumstances. "Wilson wished America to take its place in a universal society. But he was willing to participate only if the whole world acted as the United States had acted when it enjoyed isolation during the 19th century."* In reality, America, too, had entered world politics since the Spanish-American War and the building of the Panama Canal. Although Wilson, ever since he had become president in 1912, had earnestly tried to keep the United States out of world conflicts, the great European crisis of 1914 and its consequences had forced him to lead the country into the war. Strategic considerations of more than local and even more than hemispheric scope were no longer alien to American foreign policy.

But how deeply Woodrow Wilson was steeped in the political sentiment of the happy earlier period can be seen for example from his Point Four: "Adequate guarantees given and taken that national armaments will be reduced to the lowest point consistent with domestic safety." The navy "second to none" that the United States was building since 1916 could not be defined as one protecting exclusively "domestic safety," though the American peacetime army could be so described. To the continental states of Europe, land forces were their first and last line of defense. It was utterly unrealistic to ask them to be satisfied with mere frontier guards and police forces. Wilson had soon recognized this himself, and Article 8, the principal article of the League Covenant dealing with disarmament, spoke only of the reduction of national armaments to the lowest point "consistent with *national* safety and the enforcement by common action of international obligations." "Geographical situation and circumstances of each state" were to be taken into account in the formulation of the disarmament plans of the League.

---

* W. Lippmann: *U.S. War Aims* (Boston: 1944), p. 175.

These were sensible provisions. But it was unfortunate that in the meantime the German disarmament conditions imposed by the Treaty of Versailles were linked up with the future international disarmament that the League of Nations was to inaugurate. As the preamble of Part V of the Versailles Treaty put it: "In order to render possible the initiation of a general limitation of the armaments of all nations, Germany undertakes strictly to observe the military, naval, and air clauses which follow." The disarmament clauses of Versailles were no doubt a rather literal application of Wilson's Point Four, but not of Article 8 of the Covenant toward which the preamble gratuitously and mistakenly pointed.

The history of disarmament at the Paris Peace Conference can serve as a good illustration of the great distance that had to be travelled in order to translate the Wilsonian ideals into practical political arrangements. On the other hand, it offers an example of how eager Wilson was to justify concrete decisions as emanations from absolute principles. There was in Wilson's philosophy, however, a grave misunderstanding of the relation between abstract ideas and power in history. Wilson was deeply convinced that the proclamation of liberal ideals in international life would everywhere rally the common man to their support. In this sense he could say to the American delegation on his way to Paris that only he, and not Lloyd George and Clemenceau, represented the people.* But in the formal sense Clemenceau and Lloyd George represented their nations more fully than Woodrow Wilson. He had lost control of Congress in the November elections, and it was unpredictable what opposition his foreign policy might meet at home in the future. In contrast, Lloyd George had called for British elections in December and had gained a strong, if unwieldy, parliamentary majority, while the French Chamber of Deputies had voted 4:1 in favor of Clemenceau after he presented on December 27, 1918, his plans for French policy at

---

* C. Seymour: "Versailles in Perspective," *Virginia Quarterly Review*, (1943), Vol. XIX, pp. 481–97.

the approaching peace conference. Clemenceau was openly hostile to Wilsonian idealism, and the British "khaki elections" were fought by Lloyd George and his liberal and conservative party friends with nationalistic slogans that contradicted the Government's official acceptance of the Wilsonian program. The Asquith-Grey liberals, who from 1906 to 1916 had dominated British policy and in whose circles many of the Wilsonian ideas had been born, were crushed by the jingoistic temper of the British election campaign.

Still, Wilson's program appealed to the common man, and the popular ovations that he received everywhere he went in Europe were genuine. To almost everybody it seemed that the program offered a way to end the cruel bloodshed and to cure the wounds that four years of war had inflicted on all national societies. It promised gains to all the Allied powers, at the same time promising Germany as well as Austria and Hungary the protection of the principle of nationality. The Wilsonian program had a twofold root and double purpose. It was not only a design of an international peace settlement but also an instrument of political warfare. And as a political weapon it proved a complete success during 1918. It gave hope to the Allied nations in the early months of the year when they reeled under the blows of the German spring offensive in the West, it rallied the separatistic national movements in the Habsburg empire to the support of the Allied cause, and it strengthened the peace sentiment in the enemy countries. American political warfare made a great contribution to the early winning of World War I.

But the immediate impact of American propaganda on Europe was the strengthening of national sentiment. To gain or regain full national independence and the strongest possible military strength to defend it was the dearest objective of every warring European nation. The internationalism of Wilson was shared by the European statesmen only in so far as it did not deny them the full realization of their own nationalistic aims. In Wilson's eyes national self-

determination was a means to lay grievances to rest and
thus a direct step towards a peaceful international society.
To most Europeans the satisfaction of their national dreams
was an absolute end, even when their realization violated
the national self-determination of others.

Shortsighted as this policy was—and more will be said
about it later—the desire of the European states, old and
new, to gain national security through a maximum of
power, which they measured by area and population, was
to some degree understandable. As early as January, 1917,
Wilson had proclaimed that there should be no "new
balance of power," but instead a "community of power."
His concept of a League of Nations, however, though it
envisaged the ultimate use of force against an aggressor,
rested chiefly on the belief that a united world opinion
would act as a deterrent to aggression and that, if this
failed, an aggressor could probably be brought to heel by
economic boycott and blockade. Collective military action
was to be taken, if at all, only after considerable damage
had been done. Yet defense against invasion was still a vital
problem that the individual states alone or in groups would
have to meet. Although Wilson was right when he judged
that the balance of power had failed to provide a secure
foundation for world peace, the different nations, including
the United States and Britain, were far from ready to
pool their whole strength in a single "community of
power," and the relative balance of power between states
remained a matter of vital significance. The League of
Nations of 1919 was not what its English name said it was,
a closely united group of states ready for immediate concerted action. The French name *Société des Nations* described the nature of the organization more aptly.

If the League of Nations was to gain true life, its
roots had to sink deeply into the soil of national security
interests. Such a policy would have required the frank recognition of the balance of power that Wilson rejected. In
his opinion the struggle for power had come to an end
with the armistice, and the peacemakers should now settle

all claims largely on the basis of universally valid principles. Such an attitude was bound to lead to great embarrass-
ment. Inevitably, Wilson had to make continuous concessions to the balance of power. One of the first, made
shortly after his arrival in Europe, was his consent to
Italy's obtaining the Brenner Pass frontier, in stark contrast
to his own Point Nine, which had demanded "a readjust-
ment of the frontiers of Italy . . . along clearly recogniz-
able lines of nationality."

To be sure, a case could be made for giving Italy a
strong strategic frontier to the north in disregard of the
quarter million Austrians living south of the Brenner if
Austria was to be joined to Germany. Even Hitler in
Mein Kampf and later on, from 1933–43, at least, accepted
the Brenner line. But the Paris conference of 1919 prohibited the *Anschluss,* and it was difficult to see why Wilson
would accept Italy's demand for the annexation of South
Tyrol yet stubbornly oppose her Adriatic claims. This concession, like that made over disarmament, which has been
discussed already, brought Wilson's high principles under
a cloud of suspicion. It was not wise to use these ideals as
the justification of actions that were plainly decisions on
power relationships and that could not be avoided if one
wanted an agreement among the powers to make peace.
By Wilson's insistence on wrapping up necessary compro-
mises in the language of general principles, his ideals lost
much of the radiance that would have made them steady
beacons in the evolution of a collective system. Abused
ideas have a tremendous aptitude for vengeance. The difficulty during the interwar period of arousing strong popular support for the forceful maintenance of the Paris settlement was largely due to the fact that the intellectual and
moral foundation of the peace appeared to be very weak.

This is not to say that all the concessions that the peace
conference made to nationalistic demands could be called
practical decisions. Actually many of them were patently
obnoxious. But the elementary longing of states for security
could not be disregarded or met only surreptitiously. Yet

it could have been pointed out to them that no European state had ever enjoyed security in isolation and that in spite of all her wars and divisions Europe had managed in the past to restore a communal life after every crisis through which she had gone. The statesmen of the Congress of Vienna had speedily welcomed France back to the European concert without neglecting to take those precautionary measures that kept France from renewing her career of Napoleonic conquest. In the absence of general wars during the later nineteenth century the existence of neutral great powers had exercised a restraining influence upon the victor in a war. But none of these curative forces seemed to have survived the holocaust of World War I in Europe.

Formerly the monarchs and nobility had formed an upper stratum of European society. No doubt, their cupidity had caused many wars, but the similarity of outlook and interest within the group had made bargaining and compromise possible. Woodrow Wilson expected that democracy would be a better maker and guarantor of peace than monarchs and noble elites. Yet this expectation was not fulfilled in 1919.

For one thing, "democratic" foreign policy was in its infancy. Prior to World War I even people in states with a popular constitution paid little attention to the actual conduct of foreign affairs except in periods of tension. Britain had the oldest tradition of parliamentary control, and the British parties, it is true, usually identified themselves with differing foreign policies. In fact British foreign policy often changed with changing parliamentary majorities. Within these limitations, however, the prime minister and foreign secretary had great freedom in the formulation and execution of foreign policy, even to the extent of concluding secret understandings. Sir Edward Grey, who became British foreign secretary in 1905-06 after the Liberal victory at the polls, decided to accept the foreign policy of his predecessor. Continuity of British foreign policy was gained by this action, but not necessarily greater popular participation. Organizations like the Union of Democratic Control and personalities like Edmund D. Morel and James Bryce attempted to arouse public interest in a fuller parliamentary and popular control of foreign affairs and particularly in the suppression of secret diplomacy,* but the movement did not make much progress in Britain. It won many adherents in the United States, however; much of the Wilsonian concept of democratic foreign policy, including his belief in "open diplomacy," stemmed from the thought of some of these British reformers.

Thus during World War I the groups of people who were able to think about international affairs competently and with a reasonable detachment from national emotions were small in all countries and demagogy could flourish. The Americans exercised a moderating influence in a good many European matters, but they were handicapped by the political death of the old British Liberal party, with which they could have established better working relations than with Lloyd George, who, though a liberal, had made himself highly vulnerable to nationalistic pressures.

Wilson might have been in a better position to modify some of the excesses of nationalism if he could have broadened the scope of the conference debates. Everybody agreed that the political world settlement would require for its support a restoration of world trade and world economy. But the American delegation was not in a position to discuss the revival of a free and stable economy in a comprehensive and systematic fashion.

Four groups of economic problems existed in 1919. There were first the urgent relief needs in the provinces of the Central Powers and the countries that they had occupied during World War I. Second, the world faced the difficulty of rehabilitating Europe's productivity and working out a program of economic development for the new eastern

---

* James Bryce raised the issue of parliamentary control first in his *American Commonwealth*. E. D. Morel attacked secret diplomacy first after the leak of the secret articles of the Anglo-French entente during the Agadir crisis. His book *Morocco in Diplomacy* (London: 1912) was republished three years later under the title *Ten Years of Secret Diplomacy*.

European states. Third, there were the problems arising from the economic transformations that had been brought about by the great expansion during the war of non-European industries and the sudden rise of the United States as the big creditor nation of the world, particularly of Europe. Fourth, there was the difficulty of making a financial settlement between victors and vanquished nations or, more correctly, between the victors and Germany, since the Habsburg empire had disappeared.

The first problems, those of relief, were met. There was some delay due to American insistence on the dissolution of the Allied economic wartime councils after the armistice. Herbert Hoover expressed the American point of view most forcefully when he said that everything should be avoided that would give even the appearance that other powers had a voice in the assignment of American resources.* Yet, although most funds and foodstuffs came from the United States, the contribution of the British Commonwealth was by no means negligible, and it was in any case politically unwise to break up the common front, at least prior to the conclusion of peace. New inter-Allied organizations were finally set up in January, 1919, under the Supreme Economic Council, over which Lord Robert Cecil presided with Herbert Hoover, who was director general of relief.

The work done under Herbert Hoover's direction and continued after the peace by American private organizations was most effectively executed. It laid the ground for a humane link between the New and the Old World, which gave all American dealings with Europe thereafter a warmer tone. Though this relief action was originally planned only as a humanitarian measure, it was soon recognized to be also a means of keeping Bolshevism from flooding central Europe. Before long the Allies decided also on a relaxation of the blockade of Germany, continuation of which they had written into the armistice of November 11, 1918, al-

* *Papers Relating to the Foreign Relations of the United States, 1918, Supplement 1: The World War,* Vol. I (Washington: 1933), pp. 616 f.

though Britain and the United States had to overcome
French hesitation and also original German resistance to
the reasonable conditional demands for the use of German
shipping and monetary funds.*

The difference between relief and rehabilitation is a relative one. No doubt, the Allied relief activities in Europe
after 1919 were of crucial significance for the restoration of
normal economic production; but European recovery proved
a process of many years, since the problems of the second
and third groups were never tackled. Wilson was aware that
it was necessary to give the political settlement an economic underpinning, but we may question whether he had
a clear conception of the way by which this could be done.
His Point Three, for instance, demanding the removal of
all economic barriers and the establishment of an equality
of trade conditions, had been a rather simple expression
of his liberal faith. But it had come under strong fire from
the United States Senate and was in these debates reinter-
preted by the Wilson Administration in such a fashion
as to become practically meaningless.

Wilson seemed, indeed, to have resigned himself to a situation that did not allow him to commit the United States
to a definite plan for the reconstruction of world economy,
much less for special projects of European recovery and
development. He did not think it politically possible to
discuss even the settlement of the inter-Allied war debts
in this light. The British, who had given their Allies as
many loans as they had received from the United States,
early proposed to study the problem of international payments, including inter-Allied debts and German reparations,
as one affecting the whole future of world economy. They
indicated, too, that they were willing to cancel some of the

---

* Cf. W. Arnold-Forster: *The Blockade, 1914–1919* (*Pamphlets
on World Affairs*, No. 17, New York: 1939). Also D. Lloyd George:
Memoirs of the Peace Conference (New Haven: 1939), Vol. I, pp.
192 ff.; J. M. Keynes: *The Economic Consequences of the Peace* (New
York: 1920), and his article on the German representative Dr. Melchior in *Two Memoirs* (London: 1949).

loans that they had made to their Allies in order to help
the war effort if their own debts received similar consideration from the United States. But the American delegation
at Paris insisted that the American war loans, as enacted by
Congress, had been made to individual states on a strict
business basis. They could be settled only by negotiations
between the United States Government and the individual
states. The discussion of inter-Allied debts was thus excluded from the peace conference, and with this decision
the opportunity was missed for rebuilding the international
economy on a stable foundation.

German reparations consequently was the only major economic problem taken up by the peace conference. In retrospect it is easy to say that nobody, including such critics
of the Versailles settlement as John Maynard Keynes or, for
that matter, such able financial experts of the German delegation as Carl Melchior, were right in their estimate of the
reparations that Germany was able to pay. Everybody over-
rated Germany's capacity, which was not surprising, since
there was no precedent for international payments of comparable magnitude. But if one thing could have been foreseen, it was the close interrelation between any international payments, whether German reparations or inter-
Allied debts, and the future development of world economy. If international trade had expanded far beyond the
volume of 1913 and if in particular the creditor nations had
been willing to receive greatly increased imports from the
debtor countries, much larger sums might have been trans-
ferred.

The attempt to set down Germany's capacity for making
financial reparations was bound to fail. Only a flexible
scheme could have succeeded. But as it was, the Allies
wanted a definitive plan of German reparations that would
take care not only of the actual war damage but also of the
debts that they had incurred in fighting Germany. Britain
was particularly anxious; for under a strict interpretation of
the definition of German reparations contained in the Lansing note of November 5, 1918, Britain could have claimed

reparations only for shipping losses, which were actually paid by the delivery of German vessels, and for the relatively small damage suffered by some English cities as a consequence of naval or air attack.

Leaving aside shipping losses, Britain could have collected only 1 or 2 per cent of German money payments. But the British representatives argued, and General Smuts finally convinced Woodrow Wilson, that war pensions could be considered civilian damages that Germany was liable to repair. The financial bill presented to Germany was thereby tripled. However, since Germany in the end paid even less than a third of the contemplated sum, the size of the reparations was not so important as their new distribution among the Allies; Britain now claimed 22 per cent.

The Paris Peace Conference failed to make systematic plans for world recovery that would have solidified their political arrangements. The Paris peace treaties were a diplomatic peace settlement similar to the Vienna settlement, though, of course, the political philosophies of the two differed. Wilson sensed that security of nationality and frontiers was not enough and that economic and social problems as well demanded the attention of modern statesmen. The creation of the International Labor Office was an indication of such awareness. Yet the depth of the revolutionary changes that World War I had caused in the social structure and attitude of nations was hidden from the view of the peacemakers.

Broadly speaking, the wars of earlier times had been wars of armies—armies of restricted, if expanding, numbers limited in their arms and equipment. But World War I had a different character. Formerly the production of arms ceased when war broke out, but after 1916 industrial mobilization became as gigantic as the military levies. The civilians were contributing as much to the war as the soldiers, and the endless casualty lists, invasions, and blockade brought the war home to every person in Europe and Russia. In other words, after 1916 World War I turned into the first modern total war. The impact of this event was greatest in Russia, which tried a total mobilization but broke down under the burden. Germany achieved a rather complete government-directed war economy, the first planned economy in modern history.

Nobody in Paris fully realized the portents of the new age. The peace conferences of Vienna and Paris can be compared in many respects. But they took place at very different moments of history. Vienna was the settlement of twenty-odd years of general war, in which the revolutionary forces had been able to modify, but not to overthrow, the old order of Europe. In contrast, the Paris conference was a first attempt at dealing with a new situation that had begun to unfold during the war itself. It was admitted that the world had become *one* world, and a League of Nations was created. But it was a weak league, and in spite of its unassuming character it had yet to gain universality of membership. The Paris Peace Conference also carried diplomatic activities into the economic and social fields, but it did so in an irregular fashion. That the conditions resulting from total war demand for their cure total diplomacy was not yet recognized. Not even today, thirty years later, is it undisputed popular knowledge.

V

EUROPE BETWEEN TWO WORLD WARS

1. THE EUROPEAN AFTERMATH

THE Paris peace treaties were considered to constitute a world settlement; but they never did. The peace conference could do little about the problems of the Far Eastern Pacific except distribute the German colonies located in that area. But of even greater consequence was its failure to deal with Bolshevist Russia. This is not to suggest that a solution of the Russian problem would have been simple or even possible in 1919. The French were stubbornly opposed to any diplomatic contacts with the Bolshevists, whom they judged to be tools of the Germans and traitors of Russian political and financial commitments to the West. Opposed, also, was Winston Churchill, then the British secretary for war. But the West was unable to intervene in the Russian civil war except by giving arms and other implements of war to the White Russian groups fighting in various parts of Russia against the Bolshevists entrenched in Moscow and St. Petersburg. Few Allied soldiers were willing to be sent to Russia, since after the German armistice everybody was convinced that the fighting was over and that Allied war aims had been achieved.

Winston Churchill, in his Boston speech of March 31, 1949, characterized the "failure to strangle Bolshevism at its birth and to bring Russia . . . by one means or another into the general democratic system" as one of the great mistakes of Allied statesmen in 1919.* This statement seems historically correct, and Churchill deserves credit for having seen in 1919 the loss and danger to Europe involved in the isolation of a hostile Russia. It still remains doubtful however, whether the policies in support of the White Russian counterrevolutionaries could ever have been successful, even if they had been conducted by the western European Governments with full unanimity and determination. Churchill himself in retrospect expressed some concern whether the White Russians could ever have won out against the Bolshevists.† Their leaders like Denikin and Kolchak were certainly not inspired by any democratic sentiment, but were outright Czarist reactionaries. Their victory would have threatened the seizure of the land by the peasants, which had taken place during the Bolshevist Revolution. Moreover, they were active collaborators with the Western powers and could, therefore, be identified as partners in the despoilment of the Russian empire, which, with the blessings of the Western powers, was deprived of all her European provinces conquered by the German army during the War. (Ultimately, the bulk of the Ukraine was regained by the Soviet Union, but some Byelo-Russian and Ukrainian regions remained under Polish and Rumanian domination.)

The attempt at intervention in Russia after World War I gave the Communist rulers in Moscow the chance to pose as the true defenders of the Russian "motherland." They have derived great strength from this role ever since. It was revealing that the Soviet Government appealed mainly to Russian national sentiment when it officially named the Russo-German war of 1941-5 the "great patriotic war." The Allied interventions in Russia after World War I, undertaken without any realistic plan, greatly helped to make the Bolshevist party appear as the trustee of the historic Russian state.

Lloyd George, like Woodrow Wilson, disliked the mili-

* The *New York Times*, April 1, 1949.
† W. S. Churchill: *The Aftermath, The World Crisis*, 1918–28 (New York: 1929), p. 264.

tary intervention in Russia (they both believed that it would be as self-defeating as foreign intervention in the French Revolution had proved to be more than a century ago) and he wanted to initiate diplomatic negotiations.* But in the end nothing decisive was done in 1919. The British Prime Minister was the European statesman of this period who most consistently thought about the Russian problem, though he himself was not unaffected by the general feeling of the Western world that the Bolshevist experiment would soon collapse under its own unrealistic aspirations. He realized the loss that the Western world suffered by the interruption of European trade with the new Russia. When, however, he resumed his appeal for peaceful relations with the Soviet Union at the Genoa Conference in 1922, it was already too late. Russia and Germany, the two chief opponents of the Paris settlement, had concluded the Treaty of Rapallo, which established, though originally on a tenuous basis, Russo-German co-operation.

The policy of half-hearted intervention was followed by the lukewarm policy of the *cordon sanitaire*. This policy represented the open admission of the inability of the Western powers to influence the course of Russian internal affairs except by increasing the difficulties first of the stabilization and then of the forced expansion of the Russian economy. It must be added, however, that the policy of the *cordon sanitaire* contributed to the defeat of early Soviet attempts to turn the Russian Revolution into a world revolution, although events like the German recovery in the mid-twenties and the anti-Communist turn of the revolution in China were undoubtedly more important.

The failure to integrate Russia in some fashion into a European system created serious uncertainties about the future of the Continent. To be sure, for about a decade or more after the revolution, Russia was too weak to exercise any strong direct influence on Europe beyond the ideological impact of the Third International. But the existence

* D. Lloyd George: *Memoirs of the Peace Conference* (New Haven: 1939), Vol. I, pp. 207–51.

of an independent Communist Russian state that controlled an international political movement made the whole European settlement unsafe. The Communist movement intensified everywhere the social unrest that followed in the wake of the peace settlement of Paris, and the Russian state encouraged every nation willing to resist the peace treaties of 1919.

During the nineteenth century Russia had held important non-Russian territories and had wielded great influence in general European affairs. Yet at the same time Europe had not lacked power over Russia. As has been seen, Russian expansion had been kept within certain bounds, and she had been compelled to respect international treaties. Her internal development had been heavily dependent upon foreign capital and technological advice. European ideas had deeply stirred Russian intellectual life. Even the slavophile movement in Russia cannot be understood without consideration of the impact of Western thought. Russia had been "westernized" in many respects and in this process had displayed an unusual capacity for blending her own cultural heritage with modern Western ideas. In the last third of the nineteenth century the great Russian novel and Russian music had become in their turn a leaven in western European thinking.

This political and cultural *rapprochement* between Europe and Russia came to an end with the Russian Revolution. It should be remembered, however, that Marxism is not a native Russian doctrine, though in the hands of Lenin, and even more so of Stalin, it was adapted to the circumstances and needs of a Russia plunged into chaos and misery by military defeat. The philosophy of Karl Marx is an arsenal from which many political schools can draw arms. Bolshevist theory itself has undergone considerable changes since 1917 in response to new political developments. In the early years after the October Revolution the Western powers might well have moulded the circumstances that conditioned the evolution of that theory. But this opportunity, if it ever existed, was missed. The new Soviet state grew up in isolation, yet it could not fail to exercise a disruptive influence upon the European order created in Paris, the more so since Moscow ruled not only the Russian empire, now being quickly industrialized and unified in all its parts, but also the international Communist movement.

That the Paris settlement did not become a world settlement was also owing to the withdrawal of the United States from Woodrow Wilson's great design. This withdrawal was not caused by popular dissatisfaction with the treatment meted out by the Paris peace treaties to the vanquished enemies. In so far as the Senate's opposition was more than a display of partisan spirit, it centered around the fear of seeing the United States sucked into an international system whose obligations—if they were clearly understood at all —were dreaded by many Americans. In retrospect it may be asked whether Wilson's adamant insistence on the American ratification of the full Covenant showed good political judgment. Probably even an amended and watered-down Covenant acceptable to the United States Senate would have been preferable to a Covenant rejected by it, since the United States could then have been kept in contact with the unfolding European situation.

But even the rejection of the Covenant by the United States might not have been a major catastrophe if America had backed the Mutual Assistance Pact for the Rhine settlement. Theodore Roosevelt and Senators Lodge and Knox felt that it would be better to build any future American participation in world affairs around the practical experience already gained. In their opinion the wartime alliance with the Allied nations ought to be the nucleus of any future American co-operation in international affairs.* Thus they were ready to subscribe to the Rhine pact rather than to the League of Nations Covenant. From both an American and a universal point of view, it would have been desirable to have the United States join in the establishment of a world organization for the maintenance of peace; but

* W. Lippmann: *U.S. War Aims* (Boston: 1944), pp. 160 ff.

an American guarantee of the crucial western European frontiers could have been equally decisive. In the fierce party struggle between the President and the Senate both possibilities were lost, and the subsequent neglect of international affairs makes one wonder whether or not the American people would in any case have given their support to international commitments for any length of time.

The United States withdrew from world affairs in 1920 as suddenly as it had appeared on the world scene three years before. This retreat was not complete, since the United States continued to care about a settlement of Far Eastern issues and was soon drawn again into some sort of co-operation with the European powers in financial matters. Prior to 1914, the United States had been a debtor nation—that is, foreign investments in America outbalanced American investments abroad. The liquidation of European holdings in America, however, and the big American loans to the European Allies during World War I and in the armistice period made the United States the chief creditor nation, which it has remained ever since. In the period between 1920 and 1933 the country was concerned about its European loans and investments, which greatly increased after 1925, when a seemingly stabilized Europe appeared to offer splendid opportunities for American surplus capital.

Even so, the United States after 1920 felt that it could return to its nineteenth-century insularity. Its isolationism became economic as well as diplomatic. The postwar depression led to the Fordney-McCumber Tariff of 1922, and the Hawley-Smoot Tariff of 1930 carried protection to greater heights than ever before. Indeed, all postwar tariffs, of which the American tariffs were only the most outstanding examples, tended to aim at a restoration of the prewar pattern of world economy. But this economy had been irrevocably changed by the World War; Europe could pay her debts to America only if she were allowed to send her products and goods to the United States.

Europe after 1920 was left alone to cope with her political problems. It appeared at once doubtful that she would be able to do so. Quite apart from the great financial and economic questions, which could have been solved only by world-wide arrangements, the whole European scene as envisaged by the peacemakers while they still acted in concert was drastically changed by America's withdrawal. France was immediately affected. She had foregone her demands for a separation of the Rhineland in exchange for an Anglo-American guarantee of the demilitarization of the left bank of the Rhine. The great French concessions at the Peace Conference now seemed to have been made in vain.

France was particularly alarmed by the British refusal to sign the mutual guarantee pact. It was true that the Anglo-French treaty as drafted in Paris depended on the willingness of the United States to subscribe to a parallel treaty. The British decision to drop the treaty was no breach of promise, but it was a grave error of judgment. The Rhine was the natural defense line of Britain as much as of France, as World War I had abundantly shown. If Britain declined to co-operate without reservation in the defense of the Rhine, the French had reasons to distrust the good intentions or the good judgment of British policy. Were the British, once they had achieved the full realization of their war aims—the destruction of Germany as a naval and colonial power—determined to leave the Continent unprotected? France therefore proceeded to build up a system of alliances with the eastern European states.

It was dubious from the beginning whether the new eastern states would be able to live between the Soviet Union and Germany if neither were integrated in some fashion into a European system. Actually, many people forgot Russia altogether. To them Poland seemed to have taken the place that Russia had occupied in Europe before 1914, while Czechoslovakia, Yugoslavia, and Rumania, which formed in 1920–1 alliances chiefly directed against a restoration of Habsburg rule in Hungary, were considered to constitute a substitute for the Habsburg empire. But neither this group of states, called the Little Entente, nor Poland could compare to the former Habsburg or Romanov empires.

It must suffice here to mention only a few of the major weaknesses of the new eastern states. Since they looked in many different directions, toward the Baltic, the Adriatic, Aegean, and Black Seas, they had not much unity among themselves. Furthermore, the Habsburg empire, in spite of its pernicious internal controversies, had formed a viable economic entity, but the new states were confronted with unsolvable economic problems in addition to their formidable political difficulties. Of them all, Czechoslovakia was the most democratic and prosperous. Practically none of the others ever acquired an economic or political equilibrium. They were driven to adopt governmental methods that had only a superficial resemblance to democracy, and their living standards remained far below the European average. The ensuing social crisis, brought to a head by the depression of the late twenties, again inflamed the conflict of nationalities. Not only did states like Poland and Czechoslovakia continue to be at loggerheads, but issues of nationality also undermined the internal cohesion of these two countries as well as Yugoslavia. Hungary, smarting under her defeat, kept revisionist forces alive with the support of fascist Italy.

Consequently, it was an illusion to conceive of the Little Entente and Poland as substitutes for the empires of the Romanovs and Habsburgs. Between 1887 and 1917 France had spent about sixteen billion francs in loans and investments in order to build up her Russian ally.* If she could have employed similar amounts of money to set the new eastern states on the road toward prosperity, the system of French eastern alliances might have become a strong underpinning of the European *status quo*. But the French depositor, having lost more than a quarter of all

* Cf. H. Feis: *Europe the World's Banker, 1870–1914* (New Haven: 1930), p. 51; and H. G. Moulton and L. Pasvolsky: *War Debts and World Prosperity* (Washington, D. C.: 1932), p. 426.

his foreign investments as a result of the World War, was not inclined to permit his government to conduct a bold foreign economic policy. Instead, since the new states remained economically weak, their foremost customer, Germany, continued to hold considerable power in the eastern and southeastern states.

Naturally, the military agreements between France and the eastern states were practical only as long as France was physically capable of co-operating with these allies and making a substantial contribution to their defense both against Germany and the Soviet Union. This co-operation required the disarmament of Germany at least sufficient to permit French troops to force a junction with the Czechoslovak army along a line from Metz-Diedenhofen to Eger-Pilsen. It also called for an army capable of strategic maneuver and not one almost exclusively designed for defensive operations along the frontiers of France.*

Actually, France was not in a position to uphold the treaties by her own strength, but in the years immediately following the War she seemed stronger than she really was. The postwar depression, which affected the United States and Britain very severely, hardly touched France, owing to the reconstruction work going on in the war-devastated French provinces. Moreover, although at the end of 1918 the British army and airforce were probably stronger than the French services, British armed strength was dissolved with amazing speed. In 1920, needing military strength in India, in the Middle East, and in Ireland, the British army of around 300,000 men could spare only 13,000 men for occupation duty in the Rhineland and nothing but a few battalions to help in the policing of the plebiscite areas in Upper Silesia and East Prussia, though British diplomacy had been responsible for having these plebi-

* See I. M. Gibson: "Maginot and Liddell Hart: The Doctrine of Defense," in E. M. Earle (ed.): *Makers of Modern Strategy* (Princeton: 1943), pp. 365–87. The subject would, however, deserve a fresh treatment on the basis of the many memoirs published by French generals since 1945.

scites instituted. By contrast the French army seemed powerful.

The inequality in mobilized military strength added to the air of unreality that surrounded Franco-British relations in the early years after the war. The two powers even indulged in unfriendly squabbles in the Near East. But the French were chiefly worried by the thought that with the return to a small professional army the British would be incapable of assisting them in gaining security— for them the real prize of the war. France wished to see any future war fought east of the French borders and brought to a quick decision there. If Germany could invade France again or if a war should last long enough to enable Germany to mobilize her superior manpower and industrial potential, France would be destroyed again. A simple promise by Britain, as finally offered by Lord Curzon in 1922, that she would consider any German violation of the demilitarization of the Rhineland an act of aggression seemed to Frenchmen an inadequate insurance as long as Britain did not provide military forces ready to act instantaneously with the French army in the case of any threat.

Poincaré between 1922 and 1924 attempted to employ the preponderant might of France for the achievement of a European position in which France would no longer have to rely on British support. The occupation of the Ruhr in January, 1923, was undertaken to make Germany pay reparations or, in the case of German opposition, to secure the productive resources that would recompense France. In spite of German "passive resistance" French policy was successful in finally forcing Germany to come to terms; but France, as a result of her exertions, was financially exhausted and could not impose her own conditions. American and British intervention instituted the Dawes Plan, which for a period of five years removed reparations from the agenda of European diplomacy. More important, France recognized that she could not conduct an independent European policy, but would have to act in close co-operation with Britain, even at the sacrifice of some French advantages and hopes.

It is doubtful that Britain after World War I had a clear conception of the future of Europe. In less than a year after the signing of the Treaty of Versailles she developed, if not a new European policy, at least a new attitude toward European problems. Britain had been severely jolted by her inability, in conjunction with her European allies, to bring the war against the Central Powers to a victorious conclusion. America's intervention had been necessary to decide the war, and the United States proposed to maintain thereafter a navy of a size equal to the British navy. The withdrawal of the United States from European affairs was profoundly alarming to Britain, and the new world situation seemed to make it unwise to assume international obligations as far-reaching as those she had accepted prior to 1914.

The strong support that Britain had received from her dominions during the War had created a warm feeling of unity among the members of the British Commonwealth of Nations; but the British dominions were even more deeply disturbed by America's refusal to join in the guarantee of the Paris settlement than Britain herself. They contributed to the watering down of the Covenant's provisions for automatic sanctions and kept warning Britain against involvement in the problems peculiar to Europe. The exact influence of dominion opinion on British foreign policy would be difficult to measure, since Britain had reasons of her own for keeping aloof from European engagements. In the 1930's one could not help feeling that the British Government often used the dominions as an easy excuse for its own lack of decision in European affairs. Actually, the policy of the British dominions went through an evolution toward collectivism in international affairs, largely as a reaction to Japanese and Italian expansionism.*

* Cf. G. M. Carter: *The British Commonwealth and International Security* (Toronto: 1947).

Although the Commonwealth became after World War I sentimentally more important to Britain than the full participation in a European political system, obvious security needs and economic necessity made it impossible for her to withdraw from the European continent. European recovery was an absolute prerequisite for the restoration of a prosperous British economy, which, in turn, hinged on the revival of German productivity. At the same time, under the leadership of the great economic thinker John Maynard Keynes the British underwent a sudden and violent revulsion from the Paris Peace Treaties. Keynes' treatise *The Economic Consequences of the Peace Treaty*, brilliantly penned, produced an instantaneous and profound public reaction as few political pamphlets in history have ever achieved. Most British people soon agreed that the most serious problems "were not political or territorial but financial and economic, and that the perils of the future lay not in frontiers and sovereignties but in food, coal and transport." * Yet this judgment was at best a dangerous half-truth; political security and economic prosperity were equally important and interdependent. Keynes claimed more inside knowledge of the political workings of the Paris Conference than he actually possessed, and his anger at the economic errors that the conference had committed carried him into acrimonious accusations that defeated some of his own aims. He considered, for example, Anglo-American co-operation a pre-condition of world recovery. But his venomous portrait of Woodrow Wilson

* J. M. Keynes: *The Economic Consequences of the Peace* (London: 1919), p. 134. Some of the chapters suppressed by the author in 1919 were published in his *Essays in Biography* (London: 1933). The *Consequences* were followed by J. M. Keynes: *A Revision of the Treaty* (London: 1922). During World War II an able young French economist, E. Mantoux, reviewed the role played by Keynes and his writings in the history of reparations. His *The Carthaginian Peace or The Economic Consequences of Mr. Keynes* (New York: 1946) showed up many of the political and economic inconsistencies of Keynes' teachings on reparations. But he remained unconvincing in his absolute defense of the Versailles reparation settlement.

gave Wilson's American opponents additional weapons with which to defeat the League. The objective strength of the book lay in its criticism of the reparation problem, but one cannot say that Keynes displayed omniscience in all of his economic evaluations and predictions. To the British people, who had achieved all their national war aims at the Paris Peace Conference, political questions may have appeared insignificant; but for France the safety of her eastern frontiers constituted the supreme cause of anxiety and she tended to disregard the economic future of Germany. We have seen already, however, how the consequences of the Ruhr invasion compelled the French to pay heed to the economic realities of Europe; the events of 1923-24 equally forced the British Government to modify its policy. Although the sudden dismay with the peace settlement as far as it applied to the Continent of Europe caused the British nation to assume a very critical attitude towards French policy, the official British opposition to the French defense of the peace treaties could never be of a radical nature. Britain, too, wanted to extract reparations from Germany. Moreover, Britain was in no position to police Europe and had to rely on the French army for the protection of the area of the Continent strategically most vital for British security, the Lowlands and northern France. The British Government found it wise in 1922 to offer to France in the place of the abortive Rhine pact of 1919 a guarantee of her eastern frontiers that Lord Curzon called "the outer frontiers" of Britain.* Britain felt so safe in these years that the British Foreign Secretary could call the proffered guarantee a gracious "gift" to France, although it did not offer any special British contribution to the maintenance of peace. Not even Anglo-French staff conversations comparable to those held before 1914 were contemplated. The provisions of the Versailles Treaty with regard to the demilitarization of the Rhineland were not altogether forgotten in

---

* *Papers Respecting Negotiations for an Anglo-French Pact,* France No. 1 (1924), Cmd. 2169, p. 133.

the draft treaty of 1922, but Lord Curzon told the French ambassador, Count St. Aulaire, that he did not think the British cabinet "would be moved to go in substance at all outside the boundaries of the Treaty of 1919." *

In these circumstances the French saw no advantage in the conclusion of the proposed Anglo-French treaty. They felt certain that in the case of a German attack against the French frontiers Britain would be forced to come to the assistance of France, since British self-interest, created by geography rather than mere sympathy with France, would compel the British Government to adopt this course of action. Yet without prior agreement on joint military measures to be employed in such an event, both the Rhine and northern France might be overrun before British intervention could take place. The British army estimates of this period never envisaged the possible need for a British expeditionary force to be sent to the Continent.† Small wonder the French were at a complete loss to understand why their political reasoning should be deemed overlogical in Britain.

2. THE SEARCH FOR EUROPEAN SECURITY

WHILE these bilateral negotiations took place, another approach was chosen to explore solutions of the problem of security through the League of Nations. This policy was championed in Britain chiefly by the Liberal and Labor parties, though it had the support of some eminent members of the Conservative party, such as Lord Cecil. In this British school of thought Wilson's ideas found faithful apostles and followers. They were convinced that

* Ibid., p. 153. Cf. W. M. Jordan: *Great Britain, France, and the German Problem, 1918–1939* (London: 1943), probably the best monographic study of European diplomacy of the 1920's available.

† Jordan: *Great Britain, France, and the German Problem,* p. 155 f.

bilateral and multilateral alliances would lead only to a new division of the world into armed camps, whereas world peace could be made secure only in a universal system that would establish and extend the rule of law. In order to avoid war it was necessary to eliminate its potential causes, which were found in various facts of international life—the differences between the "haves" and "have-nots," the political inequality of the victorious and vanquished nations of 1919. Above all, they thought, disarmament constituted the sure road to the general pacification of the world.

Frenchmen did not share the British belief in disarmament as a step to security. The League of Geneva was almost exclusively an Anglo-American brainchild. The French plan, defeated at the Paris Conference and dubbed by Woodrow Wilson "international militarism," * aimed at assembling preponderant military power against any nation that would challenge the European order established by the Paris peace treaties. After America's refusal to join, France was even more determined to turn the League into an armed organization for the defense of the *status quo*.

The Covenant, particularly as it was interpreted by most of its members, proposed to deal with threats to the peace or actual breaches of the peace primarily through obligatory conference; for the British felt that the war of 1914 could have been avoided if the European powers had agreed to confer on the Austro-Serbian conflict. The League was supposed to place all international disputes under the review of an international conference. It could then proceed to impose sanctions or even go to war against the recalcitrant member or nonmember, provided the League Council unanimously agreed; but in the absence of unanimity the individual members regained their freedom of action, which included the right to go to war. To fill this gap and to make League action against aggression automatic and of irresisti-

---

* D. H. Miller: *The Drafting of the Covenant* (New York: 1928), Vol. II, p. 294, quoted in Jordan: *Great Britain, France, and the German Problem*, p. 206.

ble force, France, supported by her allies, pressed for supplementary arrangements.

The first result was the Draft Treaty of Mutual Assistance of 1923, which tried to solve the problem of what constituted aggression and to array an international military force against it. The treaty, which incidentally had a great influence on the United Nations Charter, was emphatically rejected by the British Labor Government as being a militaristic document.* Instead, with the consent of the British and French Governments, the Geneva Protocol which placed the emphasis upon compulsory arbitration, was drafted in 1924. The member states of the League were to bind themselves to submit their disputes to arbitration, and refusal to accept the arbitration award was to be considered an act of aggression. The Geneva Protocol appealed to the rigid French sense of law. It seemed to contain a clear-cut definition of aggression, though from a French point of view it still left much to be desired with regard to the scope and automatic immediacy of sanctions. In the eyes of its British supporters the Geneva Protocol established arbitration as the supreme instrument of peaceful settlement, and they believed it to be so effective as to make the actual application of sanctions highly unlikely. (The Labor party remained, at least to 1934, pacifist and in favor of drastic disarmament as the chief means of general pacification.)

However, the ratification of the Geneva Protocol was refused by the new British Conservative Government, which superseded the MacDonald cabinet and in which Sir Austen Chamberlain served as foreign secretary. In his opinion the protocol committed British power to an extent that might prove unbearable. There was only one aspect of the protocol that found favor also with the British Conservatives: it was directed against any aggressor, and not against a specific nation. This feature, though confined to the strategic area of northwestern Europe, also recommended the

* Jordan: *Great Britain, France, and the German Problem*, p. 205.

Locarno Treaty of Mutual Guarantee of 1925 to the new British Government.

Before appraising the work of Locarno it is necessary to discuss both the German and the British attitude toward eastern Europe. Germany could not hope for more than co-operation with the western European powers, which, at least for economic and financial reasons, was highly desirable; but she could hope for more power in the east. Her strongest resentment against the Versailles Treaty, indeed, arose from its eastern provisions, especially those concerning the Polish corridor and Danzig, but also those affecting Austria. For eastern Europe seemed to offer opportunities for making political gains at not too distant a date. The new states were weak without exception, and in their rear there loomed the Russian colossus; since this colossus was not yet firmly on its feet, Germany could assume leadership in Russo-German co-operation, which had begun with the Rapallo Treaty of 1922.

British policy towards eastern Europe was never certain after World War I. At the time of the Paris Conference Lloyd George had already seen to it that Poland was kept within bounds defined by the principle of national self-determination; the plebiscites in the German-Polish borderlands were the most important concessions the German Government achieved in Paris. In the drafting of the statute for the Free City of Danzig, British diplomacy again greatly favored German claims. In the Polish-Russian conflict British policy had aimed at an eastern Polish boundary also grounded as much as possible on the principle of nationality. But Poland, once she was saved from the Red army by the good counsel of General Weygand and the mistakes of the Russian armies (which were probably to some extent the errors of the young Stalin), claimed territories far to the east of the Curzon line. In a conversation with Aristide Briand at Downing Street in December, 1921, Lloyd George said that "the British people were not very much interested in what happened on the eastern frontier of Germany; they would not be ready to be involved in

quarrels which might arise regarding Poland or Danzig or
Upper Silesia. On the contrary, there was a general reluctance to get mixed up in these questions in any way." And
then, in language closely akin to the tenor of Neville Chamberlain's statement of 1938 on Czechoslovakia as "that far-
away country," he added: "The British people felt that the
populations in that quarter of Europe were unstable and
excitable; they might start fighting at any time, and the
rights and wrongs of the dispute might be very hard to
disentangle. He did not think, therefore, that his country
would be disposed to give any guarantees which might in-
volve them in military operations in any eventuality in
that part of the world."*

These words reflected correctly not only British popular
sentiment but also the unwillingness of the British Government of the interwar period to lead public opinion toward
a recognition of the crucial role of the eastern states for the
future of Europe. This negative attitude prevailed in Britain till 1939 and led, logically enough, to the consideration of Germany as the major bulwark of order east
of the Rhine and worthy of receiving a certain freedom of
action there. The British bewilderment over the eastern
European conditions was a main reason for the reluctance
of British diplomacy to participate actively in the protection of the security of the eastern European states.

The historical adviser to the British foreign office, Sir
James Headlam-Morley, in a remarkable and prophetic
memorandum warned Sir Austen Chamberlain in February,
1925 that "the danger point in Europe" was not the Rhine
but the Vistula, and he went on to inquire:

Has anyone attempted to realize what would happen if
there were to be a new partition of Poland, or if the
Czechoslovak state were to be so curtailed and dis-
membered that in fact it disappeared from the map of
Europe? The whole of Europe would at once be in

* *Papers Respecting Negotiations for an Anglo-French Pact.*
Cmd. 2169, pp. 112 f.

chaos. There would no longer be any principle, meaning, or sense in the territorial arrangements of the continent. Imagine, for instance, that under some improbable condition, Austria rejoined Germany; that Germany using the discontented minority in Bohemia, demanded a new frontier far over the mountains, including Carlsbad and Pilsen, and that at the same time, in alliance with Germany, the Hungarians recovered the southern slope of the Carpathians. This would be catastrophic, and, even if we neglected to interfere in time to prevent it, we should afterwards be driven to interfere, probably too late.*

Headlam-Morley argued that Great Britain could be defended only on the European Continent, irrespective of the fact that she formed at the same time the center of a world-wide empire. England had always been a part of the European political system, and most certainly so in her great days—those of Elizabeth, Cromwell, Chatham, Pitt, Castlereagh, Canning, Palmerston, Salisbury, Lansdowne, and Grey.† The British historian was also right in calling it the supreme achievement of statesmanship in the first half of the nineteenth century that France was brought back to the councils of the great European powers without being allowed to upset the order of Europe established by the Congress of Vienna. He recommended analogous concessions to Germany, particularly by a revision of reparations, but warned the British statesmen not to give Germany the chance to wreck the basic arrangements of the Paris settlement. Such sabotage would be possible, he correctly predicted, if the new eastern European states were left without general protection and if Germany were permitted to co-operate with Russia against them.

But British diplomacy, in line with prevailing public opinion in England, chose a different course. Sir Austen

* Sir James Headlam-Morley: *Studies in Diplomatic History* (London: 1929), pp. 182, 184.
† Ibid., p. 176.

Chamberlain, in spite of his strong personal sympathies for France and his suspicions of Germany, was swayed by the general sentiment that Britain could and should avoid continental entanglements except for limited commitments made for the security of the English Channel. By confining British guarantees at Locarno to western Europe, Britain gave the impression that she was willing to tolerate changes in eastern Europe, in contrast to the declared French policy.

The idea of concluding a Franco-Belgian-German pact reaffirming the Rhine settlement of Versailles and placing this pact under an Anglo-Italian guarantee originated largely in Germany. Germany was anxious to forestall any future repetition of a French invasion of the Ruhr and also to create the basis for the withdrawal of the Allied occupation forces from the Rhineland. It was obvious, however, that the Germany of 1925 could not hope to achieve revisions of the sections of the Peace Treaty of Versailles applying to the Rhine except with regard to the occupation terms, and the German foreign minister Gustav Stresemann found a majority in support of his Locarno policy among the Germans largely because it was hoped that the treaty would open the gates for a revision of the Versailles Treaty in the East.* To be sure, Germany had to sign arbitration treaties with Poland and Czechoslovakia, and France strengthened her own political ties with the two states by concluding alliances with them simultaneously with the signing of the Locarno Treaty of Mutual Guarantee. But the eastern security settlement was not reinforced by a British guarantee. Moreover, Germany, in a special protocol, was assured by the other Locarno powers that her co-operation in the defense of the League Covenant

* Stresemann's close political friend and successor, Julius Curtius, wrote with reference to the Hague Conference of 1929: "In the liquidation of the War the differentiation between West and East that we had already successfully struggled for at Locarno had to be maintained." J. Curtius: *Sechs Jahre Minister der Deutschen Republik* (Heidelberg: 1948), p. 100.

against a Russian infraction would take into account her "military situation" as well as "geographical situation."* Germany was thus deliberately given great latitude to determine her relations with Russia without much reference to her League obligations. When in April, 1926, Germany concluded the Treaty of Berlin with the U.S.S.R., providing for neutrality in case of an unprovoked attack by other powers against either signatory, Stresemann could tell the Soviet Government that the question of whether or not the U.S.S.R. would be judged an aggressor by the League of Nations in the event of a conflict with a third state "could only be determined with binding force for Germany with her own consent." †

The Locarno treaties and Germany's entrance into the League have often been described as the apogee of the international system of 1919. In reality Locarno did not create a secure foundation of a European peace. It covered up certain deep cracks that had appeared in the building, but failed to repair the structural weaknesses. It would have been desirable, and in any case unobjectionable, to make concessions to Germany between 1924 and 1930 in such matters as the occupation of the Rhineland and reparations. Probably much more should have been done to enable the young German democracy to develop under favorable conditions. But it was absolutely essential for Britain and France to keep control of any changes in Germany's position in Europe. Any revision of the Versailles Treaty should have been sought by procedures of international law and multilateral agreement and by the determined refusal of unilateral *faits accomplis*. It was a tragic fallacy to believe that eastern Europe could be neglected politically and economically without courting the

---

* A. B. Keith (ed.): *Speeches and Documents on International Affairs, 1918–37* (London: 1938), Vol. 1, p. 124. The various Locarno treaties are conveniently printed together in this volume.

† Note by the German Foreign Minister Stresemann to the Soviet Ambassador Krestinski, April 24, 1926, ibid., pp. 128 ff.

gravest dangers. Even worse was the unfounded belief that international conflicts would dissolve if the states scuttled their armaments.

It has been mentioned already that the new eastern European states did not possess sufficient unity among themselves. Nor was this lack of unity among them surprising, since they had developed in different directions as borderlands of the historic European community. For a time the Habsburg monarchy had bound the nationalities of the Danube basin together, and this Austria had been a major force in the maintenance of a European order. But once the Turkish pressure subsided and democratic national movements raised their heads, the Habsburg empire was doomed. No doubt, the establishment of some sort of Danubian federation after 1919 would have been desirable for many reasons, but it alone would not have solved the decisive problems of security of the new eastern states. They could have found a solution only within a closely integrated European system, which the League of Nations and the European diplomacy of the interwar period failed to provide.

The fragile nature of the political conditions of Europe was further endangered by the pious hope that international disarmament by itself constituted a means for the creation of greater security. Large sections of the British people entertained this expectation with an almost religious fervor, and America gave their aspirations strong moral support. But in spite of the idealism of these sentiments, which deserved respect, they were utterly incapable of improving the actual political conditions of Europe. There disarmament could only mean the disarmament of the victors and new strength for Germany. In the absence of ready and fully equipped armed forces elsewhere, the superior industrial and manpower resources of Germany were bound to become even higher trumps than they were before. It would even have been preferable to raise the level of German armaments by international agreement, rather than demand the curtailment of the French army.

In most cases disarmament was claimed to be the cure of Europe's political ills by the very people who wanted all nations to accept the rule of international law. But they did not admit what is a truism in national life, that unenforceable law becomes a mockery of justice. Who was to protect the eastern states against Germany or against a revived Russia? Who was to defend western Europe, including the Lowlands and Great Britain, against the onrush of a remilitarized Germany, possibly abetted by Russia? Only one lonely European statesman warned the world that the French army was the single stabilizing factor in Europe and that "the sudden weakening of that factor of stability . . . might open floodgates of measureless consequences in Europe at the present time, might break the dyke and 'Let the boundless deep/Down upon far off cities while they dance—/or dream.' " *

But the British people were not inclined to listen to Winston Churchill in those years. From 1926 to 1934, first on the Preparatory Commission for the Disarmament Conference, then at the Disarmament Conference itself, which started its sessions in Geneva in 1932, steady pressure was brought on France to decrease her armaments. Even after Hitler's accession to power, Ramsay MacDonald pushed a disarmament plan that would have equalized French and German armed strength. France in British eyes appeared petulant in her insistence upon a system of general security or at least upon international arms inspection as preconditions of a further reduction of armaments. The result of all the disarmament discussions in the interwar period was the further discredit of the peace settlement of 1919 and the psychological preparation of a large segment of world opinion for German rearmament.

Locarno did not lay a safe foundation of a lasting European peace, though it created, at least for a while, closer co-operation between Germany and the two western European powers. The personal relationship established between

* *House of Commons Debates*, June 29, 1931, col. 936, quoted in Jordan: *Great Britain, France, and the German Problem*, p. 162.

Sir Austen Chamberlain, Aristide Briand, and Gustav Stresemann gave Europe a kind of unofficial council that tended to stabilize the European scene in spite of continuous German desire for change. Besides, for the time being Germany was in no position to press her claims for revision at the expense of eastern countries. Nevertheless, Great Britain, though she had refused to guarantee the eastern states, feared eastern conflicts. Consequently, British diplomacy chose the easy course and backed the strongest power, France.* As late as 1931 British policy supported the French opposition to the Austro-German customs union. Once Germany had become stronger than France the eastern policies of Britain were to be reversed.

By hindsight it is easy to say that the years between 1925 and 1930 were the years in which Europe could have been reconstituted, not as an entirely self-contained political system, but as a strong powerblock in world politics if the beginnings of co-operation between Britain, France, and Germany had been carried to a full understanding on all the major issues of Europe. Such a firm understanding among the three powers could also have led to a common program for the strengthening of the eastern European states. Britain, however, was not willing to consider additional commitments in Europe. Perhaps Germany and France could have acted alone, disregarding the British sensitiveness to separate Franco-German co-operation;† but Germany felt that France would never voluntarily make those concessions that Germany considered her due and that France was aiming exclusively at bolstering the *status quo*. Briand's proposal for the formation of a European Federal Union, first broached in 1929, was too vague and did not contain special concessions that might have won over Germany. Britain poured cold water on the plan, while Germany at first took a reserved attitude. Later, in March, 1931, the German Government used the

* Cf. A. Wolfers: *Britain and France between Two Wars* (New York: 1940), pp. 265 ff.
†Jordan: *Great Britain, France, and the German Problem*, p. 199.

idea of a European federation as a cloak for the Austro-German customs union, judged by France to be a unilateral revision of the Paris settlement rather than a step in the direction of a European federation. By then the chance for real understanding was gone.

The five years after 1925 gave Europe a last Indian summer before the blizzard of the world economic crisis struck in 1931. Nobody foresaw that Europe, politically and economically, lived on borrowed time. Once confidence had been restored, Europe showed her vigor. By 1925 most nations of Europe had achieved their prewar production levels, and in the subsequent five years the expansion of European production proceeded at a faster rate than that of American production during the boom period. Most startling was Germany's progress. In 1919 her industrial production was only one third of what it had been in 1913. By 1922 a considerable recovery had taken place in spite of the instability of the German currency, which was not the result of German reparation payments, as is so often asserted, but of the inability of the German Republic to put its finances in order. The decision to meet the French invasion of the Ruhr by passive resistance and to cover the bill by the printing of money led to the German hyper-inflation that was stopped only at the end of 1923,* and in that year German industrial production fell again to 40 per cent of the 1913 figure. But in 1924 Germany doubled her output, and by 1927 she had reached her prewar position and resumed her place as the chief industrial country of Europe.

Another aspect of these five years was the ease with which Europe as a whole rebuilt her trading position, even though, while Europe had been at war, the overseas countries, primarily the United States but also other nations such as Japan, had greatly expanded their productive capacity. Higher world production seemed to find a greater world market. It was not recognized that the market con-

---

* Cf. C. Bresciani-Turroni: *The Economics of Inflation* (London: 1937), p. 93.

ditions were largely the result of the credit expansion caused by American capital looking for profitable investment. The foreign capital issues publicly offered in the United States between 1920 and 1931 amounted to 11.6 billion dollars, of which Europe received 40 per cent, Canada almost 29, and Latin America 22 per cent.* In Europe, American capital was augmented by British, Swiss, and Dutch funds. Germany in the six years between 1924 and 1929 received from all these countries more than 4 billion dollars, about half of these funds coming from the United States and constituting a greater grant of foreign funds than the rest of the world received in those years.

The economic expansion of credit thus made it possible to postpone the adjustment to the structural changes of the world economy produced by the war. For the same reason a realistic financial settlement of the World War could be delayed for many years. The Dawes Plan of 1924 had set up a payment schedule of German reparations without, however, revising the original total sum demanded by the Allies in 1921. The stillborn Young Plan of 1929, announced as the final reparation settlement on the eve of the big crash, once again evaded the most fundamental political problems. Germany, beginning in 1926, paid 10,333 million German marks as reparations, which was a little less than two and a half billion dollars. But the transfer of German funds could not have been made if private American loans had not gone to Germany at the same time. The Allies in turn used these sums to service their American loans or war debts. Winston Churchill called this system "insane." †

Once the bubble burst and it dawned upon the world that there had been general overproduction and overinvestment, the American Government preferred virtually to stop all intergovernmental debts, reparations, and inter-

* J. B. Condliffe: *The Commerce of Nations* (New York: 1950), p. 447.
† W. S. Churchill: *The Second World War: The Gathering Storm*, Vol. I (Boston: 1948), p. 9.

Allied obligations in order to save the American private loans that more directly affected the American banking situation. President Hoover proposed in 1931 a holiday of reparation and inter-Allied debt payments. In 1932 at the Conference of Lausanne reparations were actually buried.* But at that time Germany was already determined not only to demand a radical revision of the Paris settlement in her favor but to force a full reversal of the historic decisions of World War I.

* Cf. J. W. Wheeler-Bennett: *The Wreck of Reparations* (New York: 1933); also C. R. S. Harris: *Germany's Foreign Indebtedness* (London: 1935).

VI

WORLD WAR II

1. HITLER'S WAR

THE Great Depression of 1931–3 demonstrated again that Europe had ceased long ago to be the ruler or chief mover of world economy. The crisis was a world crisis; its first signs appeared in the United States in 1929 and were at once reflected most sharply in the precariously balanced German economy. The national income table of the United States fell from 100 in 1929 to around 50 in 1932, while in Germany it declined to 60 and in Britain to around 85.* The world economic crisis had great, and in some respects disastrous, social consequences in Europe, but only in those countries in which internal social and political struggle was ripe.

Great Britain not only made a good recovery but raised her national income table to 120 by 1938, whereas the United States recovered only to around 85 by that year. In Britain by 1935 the national income was restored to the level of 1929, in Germany by 1938, and in the United States not until 1941. On the whole, the depression was milder and the recovery greater in Britain than in other countries. Only Norway, New Zealand, and to a lesser degree Sweden made a similar recovery. It was understandable

* The most impressive graphic presentation of the world economic crisis in terms of world trade was given by the League of Nations: *World Economic Survey*, 1932–33 (Geneva: 1933), p. 8, reproduced in Condliffe: *The Commerce of Nations*, p. 495.

that to a trading nation such as Britain recovery became
the major preoccupation. The pound devaluation of 1931
and the departure from the gold standard saved the whole
British banking structure and laid the basis for a favorable
development of British trade. But Englishmen doubted that
their financial position could be defended another time
against such pressure as the crisis of 1931 imposed on
Britain and her empire. Great caution became the characteristics of British policy.

Among the great events of British history was the transformation of the old British empire into the modern British Commonwealth, which began in the free co-operation of
World War I and culminated in the Statute of Westminster
of 1931. The British dominions, Canada, New Zealand,
Australia, South Africa, and Eire are now at complete
liberty to conduct their own foreign affairs. This principle
is not an academic theory, as Eire's policy before and during World War II has shown. On the other hand, Eire
aside, the Statute of Westminster was not the result of a
revolt of the dominions against the mother country, nor
was it reluctantly granted by Britain. The statute was
founded on the belief that Britain and the dominions, by
working together in full independence, would be able to
forge an even more unified policy in world affairs than
under the empire.

This expectation has been amply justified by the history
of the last twenty years, during which the British Commonwealth has proved to be a most effective model league
of nations. At the same time, however, the harmonious relations between the members of the new Commonwealth
have further strengthened the relative aloofness of Britain
from the Continent, the more so since economic recovery
has also been closely linked to the dominions and colonies.
Britain gave up free trade principles when in 1932 she negotiated the Ottawa agreements, which established prefer-
ential tariffs for the British dominions and colonies. Furthermore, British economic prominence over the Continent
has never been fully restored. Indeed, Britain has not

seemed entirely disinclined to let other powers take leadership of the Continent, provided that they would do so in
a peaceful manner and with due respect to the vital British interests in western Europe.

Although the Great Depression did not cause any social
disturbances in Britain, it brought into the open the grave
internal conflicts latent in France and Germany. The depression hit France about a full year later than the rest of
Europe. Though an exact comparison is impossible, it is
probably correct to say that the economic dislocation in
France was not so severe as in Britain and Germany,
largely owing to her greater economic self-sufficiency. Still,
full recovery was never achieved. After World War I the
state of France had called for drastic readjustments, but
they were never firmly tackled. A reform of the French
tax system, for example, was overdue both for financial
and social reasons but was postponed in the hope of German reparation payments. Even after 1932 French public
finances remained in disorder, while the French franc, instead of following the British pound, was vainly defended
at a high level detrimental to French trade. Unemploy-
ment was fought by the repatriation of millions of Italian
and Polish workers who had come to France after World
War I and represented manpower that should have been
considered a valuable asset, considering the falling birth-
rate.

The consequences of the economic crisis were felt through
the thirties, and they helped to magnify the sharp political
rifts that beset the Third Republic. The democratic forces
were divided by the issue of socialism. Reaction on the
right used the fascist groups that sprang into being during
these years, while on the left a strong Communist party
arose. The gravity of the internal struggle was reflected in
the conduct of French foreign policy. The instability of
French parliamentary government with its continuous cabinet changes was by itself a serious handicap to a steady
and firm presentation of French external interests. The
deep ideological divisions that separated the various politi-

cal and social parties of France made them susceptible to the catchwords and ruses of propaganda emanating from the new centers of totalitarianism, Rome, Berlin, and Moscow.

French policy tried to meet the threat of Hitler Germany by measures of orthodox diplomacy; she turned to the Soviet Union for help in restoring a balance of power. Russia, which since 1928 had been bent upon the expansion of her productive capacity, was alarmed by the Japanese aggression in Manchuria and the appearance of a belligerently anti-Bolshevist Germany. During 1931-2 she began to modify her foreign policy by concluding a number of non-aggression treaties with Poland and the Baltic countries, and in 1934 she entered the League of Nations. The establishment of diplomatic relations by the United States in 1933 was welcome, particularly in view of Japan's threat. Simultaneously with these steps in diplomacy, Comintern policy was revised. Communist strategy had prescribed absolute opposition to democratic forms. The German communists, loyal to this principle, had done their best to wreck the German Republic, thus clearing the path for Hitler, but the fall of the German Republic led to a change in Communist tactics. The Communist parties were urged to join forces with any group ready to fight fascism. This policy received its first great test in France, where from 1936-8 a Popular Front Government held power.

The Franco-Soviet Mutual Assistance Pact was signed in May, 1935 and ratified by the French Chamber of Deputies in February, 1936. The long delay in the ratification indicated that the pact was not received with enthusiasm in France. The French Right disliked Russia, and its opposition to the pact became very vociferous when the Popular Front Government could be accused of carrying Soviet influence into home affairs. Passionate partisanship aside, many Frenchmen doubted that the Russia of the purge trials was a strong military ally. It seemed questionable whether the Franco-Soviet Pact was practical from the French point of view. The agreement was not well re-

ceived in Britain nor in Italy, but even more serious was
the loss of confidence in French diplomacy in the allied
countries of Yugoslavia and Poland. The latter, disappointed at France's feeble reaction to the rise of the Nazis,
had already signed a non-aggression treaty with Germany
in the spring of 1934. Only Czechoslovakia followed the
French example and concluded a pact with the Soviet
Union. In all, the Franco-Soviet Pact proved more of a
liability in the domestic and foreign policies of France
than a real gain.

France tried at the same time to form closer ties with
Italy, which, while German might was still growing to full
stature, gained for a few years the position of a quasi-
great power. For a decade Italian fascism had been a considerable influence in undermining the peace settlement
and the democratic belief on which it was grounded. In the
Balkans and southeastern Europe, Mussolini's policy had
been rather obnoxious. Still, Italy was, as Arnold J. Toynbee has called her, only a "would-be great power," and
there were, in addition to the political, very strong economic reasons for not offending common international
morals too greatly. Furthermore, Hitler's attempt to annex
Austria, initiated almost immediately after he had assumed
power and culminating in the murder of Chancellor Doll-
fuss in July, 1934, made Italo-German relations tense. Mussolini saw a major Italian interest in the preservation of an
independent Austria. A Greater Germany at the Brenner
Pass would be able, he rightly assumed, to command
Italy. Thus Italy undertook to protect the outward au-
tonomy of Austria, though Mussolini insisted on the suppression of her democratic parties. The Austrian issue
brought Italian policy into contact with French diplomacy
and also induced Italy to subscribe to the paper declarations against German rearmament.

Now that Germany's might had begun to impress France
and Great Britain, Italy won new freedom of action and
a bargaining position between Germany and the western
European powers. Thinking that there was still time for

Italian imperial conquests before Hitler acquired a dominant role in Europe, Mussolini plunged into the conquest of
Ethiopia, but he thus unintentionally strengthened Germany. He was encouraged by the French readiness to satisfy some of the Italian claims for colonial compensation,
which had been hanging fire since the Peace Conference of
Paris. No historian will ever be able to penetrate the mind
of the shifty Pierre Laval, but it is likely that he nodded
assent when Mussolini intimated his Abyssinian plans. The
Italian aggression in the Red Sea region aroused British
public opinion, however. Britain, which had held her hands
before her eyes in the Italian attack on Greece during the
Corfu crisis of 1923 and had been unwilling to enforce
the League Covenant against Japan for invading Manchuria, suddenly demanded collective action against Italy.
Formerly France had championed "putting teeth into the
Covenant." Now she could not very well oppose the British wish to use the few sanctions that the Covenant had
envisaged. The application of sanctions was bound to im-
peril the containment of Nazi Germany, which had just announced the introduction of universal military service and
the establishment of an air force.

The British Government recognized that collective action
against Italy necessitated concessions to Germany. With a
complete disregard of France and of earlier statements of
British policy, Sir Samuel Hoare offered Germany the
naval agreement of June, 1935, which scrapped the terms
of naval disarmament of the Versailles Treaty and indirectly excused Hitler's violation of the land disarmament.
This high-handed British action had a demoralizing effect
on France and made her drag her feet during the League
actions against Italy. Furthermore, official British policy
showed little determination to push sanctions the whole
way. The Suez Canal was not closed, nor were oil sanctions imposed. Both measures might have had to be backed
by force, and Britain shied away from any warlike ges-
ture. In December, 1935, Hoare and Laval drafted a plan
for the settlement of the Ethiopian war that provided for

great concessions to the Italians,* though it was more than doubtful that Mussolini would have accepted the plan. The project was killed, however, by the British people, who had been aroused to put their trust in the Covenant and had been made to believe that the British Government was executing its provisions scrupulously. On the other hand, the vast majority of British supporters of the League were not prepared to go to war against Italy, and thus the Italians, armed with mechanized weapons and poison gas, could complete their conquest of the Abyssinian empire.

The final outcome of these political events was frightful. The actual and moral authority of the League was spent. If Mussolini had been defeated, it would have served as a strong warning to Hitler; but the tomfoolery of the western powers finally drove Mussolini into the arms of Hitler. In July, 1936, Austria's Chancellor Schuschnigg was forced to conclude an agreement with Hitler that was the opening wedge for the Nazi penetration of Austria. Italian acquiescence was the price paid by Mussolini for the formation of what became known as the Rome-Berlin Axis.

The rise of German power, signalized by these last events, was to a large extent the result of the German re-militarization of the Rhineland in March, 1936. Acting against the advice of the conservative leaders of the German army, Hitler had marched German troops to the left bank of the Rhine in violation of those articles of the Versailles Treaty that had been reaffirmed at Locarno. The "caretaker" Government then in power in France had failed to react except by expressions of moral indignation. If France had sent her troops into the Rhineland or at least into the Saar, she still could have defeated Hitler's designs and forced the hands of British diplomacy; but she had been no longer confident of her own strength and had been used to acting in concert with Britain. Britain, again grown highly critical of France during the

---

* See the map in C. E. Black and E. C. Helmreich: *Twentieth Century Europe* (New York: 1950), p. 610.

Ethiopian crisis, had been inclined to condone any German move directed toward the attainment of German "equality." That Hitler rightly diagnosed the confusion of mind existing among the western powers explains these early successes, which before long placed the fate of Europe in his hands.

Hitler succeeded in showing up the utter futility of French policy in Europe. After the military reoccupation of the Rhineland effective French military co-operation with the eastern European states was made increasingly difficult in direct proportion to the further progress of German rearmament. The whole French system of alliances and guarantees clearly became an overextension of French policy and strategy. In 1938 the French had to beg Britain to liberate them of their commitments to Czechoslovakia.* In 1939 they considered their Polish ties merely a means of buying a breathing spell for the building of a western front. The Rhineland crisis of 1936 broke all French aspirations for leadership in European affairs. Thereafter France trailed British diplomacy, and in so far as she exerted any influence of her own, she produced an even greater "appeasement" of Germany than Britain was willing to practice. France had no longer the will to be a great power, although she still commanded the greatest land force that could be pitted against Germany. (Since 1929, however, when France had decided upon the construction of the Maginot line, the French army had become exclusively a force for the defense of the soil of France.)

Hitler's first political ideas were formed in Austria in the heated struggle of nationalities that ushered in the final disintegration of the Habsburg empire. He belonged to those Germanic lower middle-class groups in Austria that felt that the Austrian Government was selling out to the non-Germanic peoples of the empire. These groups culti-

---

* J. W. Wheeler-Bennett: *Munich, Prologue to Tragedy* (London: 1948), pp. 103–4.

vated racial nationalism as a religion and saw in Germany
the true and only representative of the Germanic mission
for world rule. As an anti-Semitic and anti-Habsburg pan-
Germanist, Hitler removed himself to Germany shortly before World War I and enlisted in the German army in
August, 1914.

Hitler came from the social stratum that comprised the
truly rootless and homeless elements of the capitalistic society. It is usually assumed that the proletariat constituted
the disinherited group, and it is true that it carried the
greatest social burden. But the European labor movement
imbued the individual worker with a sense of human comradeship and a faith in the future of his class. The "little
man" just above the proletariat, however, did not share
the proletarian pride, nor did he participate in the com-
forts of a bourgeois existence and in its cultural achievements. He tended to look at the existing order in purely
materialistic terms and to set up secular beliefs such as
race superiority as his pseudo-religion. Hitler was the true
exemplar of a socially and morally shiftless group. Un-
successful in his professional ambitions and without
friends, the army life gave him for the first time the sense
of belonging to a group and having a useful function in
the process of history.

In the years 1914–18 Hitler absorbed the spirit of the
German army, which was to him the embodiment of the
struggle for Germanic supremacy. The German defeat in
1918 was caused in his opinion by the failure of the German monarchy to make the doctrines of militaristic pan-
Germanism the exclusive law of the land. Since totalitarianism was the prerequisite for the conduct of modern total
war, the army was to provide the model for the ideal organization of the nation. In Hitler's reasoning World
War I was only the first round in the fight for the German domination of Europe. It would be a mistake to aim
at the restoration of the European world of 1914, since
this order had not given the Germans their proper place.
All people of German blood living in Europe had to be

brought together in a single Greater German *Reich*. Then German power could be directed toward the defeat of the western nations and the subjugation of the eastern states, where an expanding German race would find the additional "living space."

The Versailles Treaty was not the real object of Hitler's criticism, though a large part of his propaganda dwelt on its alleged injustices. As a passionate champion of the revision of the treaty, he found a following not only among the lower German middle classes and farmers but also among the *bourgeoisie* at large, whose strong nationalism was, however, tempered by the recognition of some moral obligations. Only the German working class and substantial Roman Catholic groups proved entirely impervious to Hitler's promises. Foreign statesmen made the same mistake as did many Germans in appraising him as the vindicator of Germany's claims for the revision of Versailles. Adolf Hitler thought of himself as a modern Genghis Khan, capable of setting the course of history for the next thousand years by the application of his absolutely amoral and ruthless willpower. To use a phrase with which Ranke once described Napoleon, he was a "beast of conquest."

His great political astuteness was undeniable. He had an uncanny sense of the weaknesses of the European order, and, since the historic Europe and its civilization meant nothing to him, he exploited them without the slightest consideration for any future consequences. Hitler was not insane, though there was a sickly and macabre air about him. He was extremely hysterical, but his hysteric fits and rages were often deliberately used to further his political ends. Although a vulgar person, he had acquired knowledge of political and military affairs.* Nevertheless, as Stalin remarked in a conversation with Roosevelt and Churchill, in which he warned the two not to underrate Hitler's ability, Hitler was not "basically intelligent," he was "lacking in culture," and he displayed a "primitive approach to po-

---

* See the analysis by F. Gilbert in his introduction to *Hitler Directs His War* (New York: 1950).

litical and other problems." * His early successes between
1933 and 1938 made the German dictator, always stub-
born, even less inclined to seek expert advice and more
and more dependent upon his "intuition." What knowledge
he had was very uneven. For example, he knew more of
France and Italy than of Britain. His judgments on the
United States displayed an abysmal ignorance, but he
showed an understanding of the Russian Bolshevist political tactics—indeed the Nazi leaders had learned a great
deal from them. But, like most non-Russian statesmen, he
underrated the actual strength of the Soviet state.

Hitler inherited important achievements of the Weimar
Republic. German foreign policy between 1919 and 1932
had already gained important revisions of the Versailles
Treaty. Even more significant, popular opinion in the former Allied countries had lost confidence in the moral basis
and in the practicality of many treaty provisions, and this
popular distrust was likely to hinder the Allied powers in en-
forcing the letter of the treaty. Germany, therefore, could
expect further concessions. But neither Britain nor France
knew where to draw the line. In fact, they had no conception of a European political system in which Germany
would have full equality of status without being able to
gain supremacy.

One British statesman presented a clear-cut program during these years; Winston Churchill did not oppose concessions to Germany except with regard to German rearmament, but he advocated the maintenance of the arms
superiority of the western powers and the creation of a
collective system of sanctions through the League of Nations.† Speaking as an historian in 1948, he asserted that
such a policy would have avoided World War II, which he
calls the "unnecessary war."‡ Churchill probably would not

---

* R. E. Sherwood: *Roosevelt and Hopkins* (New York: 1948),
p. 782.
† Churchill: *The Second World War: The Gathering Storm*,
Vol. I, p. 15 f.
‡ Ibid., p. iv.

deny, however, that there is an overriding necessity in the course of history, grounded not so much in political events as such as in the moral and intellectual fiber of nations and men. Of course, we must assume with him that statesmen have a limited choice not only of political objectives but also of methods to achieve them. Although it is doubtful that after World War I the victorious Europeans had it in their hands to restore the Continent to full prosperity without much active American co-operation, it is possible that Britain and France together could have built and upheld a European political system in spite of the withdrawal of the United States from Europe after 1920. However, the implementing of such a policy would have required statesmanship of a high order, which did not exist in the democracies during the interwar period. The opportunity for rebuilding an integrated political system in Europe, if it ever existed after World War I, had already been missed by the time that Hitler came to power.

The illogical, illusory and fainthearted policies of France and Britain enabled Hitler to wrest the initiative from the western European powers, and he started to employ his shock tactics accompanied by propaganda alternating temptation and scorn. The Spanish Civil War of 1936–39, in which Italy, Germany, and the Soviet Union intervened, gave Hitler a chance to keep the western powers worried and to demonstrate that Germany was the protector of European civilization against Bolshevism. At the same time Hitler was careful in meting out German support, since he did not wish General Franco to win too fast. He wanted to see Mussolini deeply involved in Spain so that the annexation of Austria would not meet with Italian opposition. Hitler was completely successful in his policy, which was designed to give *Il Duce* the impression that he would have full German backing in his desire to turn the Mediterranean into the Roman sea it had been in the days of the ancient Roman empire. In October, 1936, the Rome-Berlin Axis was born,* an ominous sign that Italy was no

* See E. Wiskemann: *The Rome-Berlin Axis* (London: 1949).

longer interested in Austria; in May, 1939, it was imple-
mented by a military and political alliance, the Pact of
Steel, between the two fascist powers.*

Soon after the establishment of the Rome-Berlin Axis,
the era of Stanley Baldwin and Ramsay MacDonald, who
alternately and together had governed Great Britain for
thirteen years, drew to its close.† The time was ripe for
a reassessment of Britain's position in world affairs, for
she had proved entirely unwilling and unable to live up to
the British signature of the Locarno Treaty and had shown
a wavering attitude all through the Spanish Civil War. The
affairs of King Edward VIII and the pageantry of the
coronation of George VI helped to delay a radical review
of British foreign policy; but late in May, 1937, Sir
Neville Chamberlain became prime minister and Lord Halifax lord president of the council. Anthony Eden remained
British foreign secretary till February, 1938. He favored
a stiffer policy towards the Axis powers, for his dealings
with Hitler as well as Mussolini had given him an understanding of the recklessness and mendacity of the fascist
dictators, and he placed little faith in any agreements with
them. He did not press his point of view too strongly,
however, partly because of prevailing British public sentiment and a sense of party discipline, but even more because of the appalling state of British armaments. Chamberlain's policy of appeasement dominated British diplomacy.

Chamberlain admitted the dangerous weakness of British
defenses, and he presented to the British parliament in
1937 a substantial program of rearmament, which aimed
primarily at a large expansion of the Royal Air Force.
But the program could not make Britain's defenses strong
before 1940, nor was it designed to give her the necessary

* M. Toscano: *Le origini del patto d'acciaio* (Florence: 1948).
Cf. L. B. Namier: *Europe in Decay* (London: 1950), pp. 129–44.
† Wheeler-Bennett: *Munich, Prologue to Tragedy*, p. 264. Cf.
also Churchill: *The Second World War: The Gathering Storm*, Vol.
I, p. 21.

forces to intervene decisively in Continental conflicts. As a matter of fact, only the introduction of military conscription could have given Britain that power. Yet neither Hitler's annexation of Austria nor Munich could convince Chamberlain of its necessity. Conscription was not introduced before May, 1939. Incidentally, even then Labor, the minority party, opposed it furiously. Among its ranks the curious belief that collective security was a wholesome principle, even if none of the members could provide the means to enforce it, lingered on to the eve of World War II.

Chamberlain did not believe in collective security; but neither did he put great trust in armaments. He was confident that no appeal to arms would ever have to be made if the problems that vexed Europe were met realistically in direct negotiations. Realism meant in this case the acceptance of Germany as the great power of central Europe and the satisfaction of her grievances in so far as they stemmed from the inequalities imposed upon her by the Versailles Treaty. Chamberlain thought it would be perfectly possible to make Hitler conform to peaceful methods of treaty changes, and this objective he made the mainstay of his policy.

There was some good sense in this aim, since the opposition to unilateral action by a single state and the taming of a state that would take the law into its own hands are the first steps in overcoming international chaos and preparing for the rule of international law. Nevertheless, the cause of peace and international law is not helped if the peace-loving and law-abiding states assent to a breach of law in order to avoid a "unilateral" action that is more correctly a crime. Such an agreement is an act of folly if accompanied by the actual sacrifice of the strength that alone would have been capable of defending the law.

Chamberlain never intended such a sacrifice. Though he abhorred war, there was never any doubt that he would fight if he thought the principles on which British life was built were threatened. It is questionable, however, whether he was sufficiently perspicacious to recognize the moment when Britain would be seriously jeopardized. Moreover, he and the members of his crew, like Lord Halifax, Sir John Simon, and Sir Samuel Hoare, not only hoped for peaceful international change and German reconciliation but also believed that irrespective of all moral considerations the German drive for conquest could be slowed up if Germany were allowed to make some big gains. The theory that the problem of National Socialism could be solved by "satiating" Germany was tempting, particularly since it was a solution at the expense of countries that most British people tended to consider "far-off" lands.

The medley of motives and aims of which the British policy of appeasement was composed was highly complex. The foremost error of this policy was its fallacious appraisal of Hitler. In official British thinking, German National Socialism was the old German nationalism rekindled and burning with greater heat, whereas in reality it was a militaristic pan-Germanism wedded to a complete moral nihilism. It would be unfair to blame this misunderstanding exclusively on the statesmen of the period. One might as well criticize their teachers, the historians, who taught the unbreakable continuity of national character and national interests without paying much attention to the social and moral forces that determined the true character of the policies of individual nations. The same lack of critical analysis of the source and substance of national policies explains many shortcomings in the policies of the Allied powers during World War II.

On November 5, 1937, Hitler exposed to the German military chiefs and the foreign minister, Baron Neurath, his "fundamental principles" regarding German foreign policy.* He explained to them his determination to con-

---

* The original minutes of this important meeting, written by Colonel Hossbach, are found in Der Prozess gegen die Hauptkriegsverbrecher vor dem Internationalen Militärgerichtshof, Nürnberg 14. November 1945–1. Oktober 1946 (Nuremberg: 1947), Vol. xxv, pp. 402–13. Translation in Nazi Conspiracy and Aggression (Washington,

quer the necessary "living space" for the Germanic race on the Continent even at the risk of a general war. As a preparatory move he envisaged the early annexation of Austria and Czechoslovakia, to be followed by later aggressive acts. To this program he adhered, except that he speeded up his original timetable within the next few months. The signs of a weakening of British and French opposition to radical revisions of the political map of Europe came to Hitler fast and thick.

Only two weeks after Hitler's speech before the chiefs of the armed forces at the Berlin chancellery, Lord Halifax visited Hitler at his mountain residence in Berchtesgaden to explore the possibilities for an Anglo-German agreement. Hitler was pleased to hear Germany described by Halifax as "the bulwark of the West against Bolshevism," but even more to learn that "the British did not believe that the *status quo* had to be maintained in all circumstances." And Halifax added: "Among the questions in which changes would probably be made sooner or later were Danzig, Austria, and Czechoslovakia. England was only interested in seeing that such changes were brought about by peaceful development."* Yet Neville Chamberlain was apparently not discouraged by the report that Lord Halifax brought back from Germany. In February, 1938, Lord Halifax replaced Anthony Eden in the Foreign Office; in Germany Hitler himself took over the war ministry, appointed to the army command generals more subservient than General Fritsch, and awarded the foreign ministry to Ribbentrop. Thus strengthened, Hitler overwhelmed Austria on March 12, 1938.

The annexation of Austria as such was not deplored by

D. C.: 1948), Vol. III, document 386–PS, pp. 295–305, and also *Documents on German Foreign Policy, 1918–1945*, Series D (1937–1945) (Washington, D. C.: 1949) Vol. I, pp. 29–39. Cf. F. Hossbach: *Zwischen Wehrmacht und Hitler, 1934–38* (Wolfenbüttel-Hannover: 1949).

* *Documents on German Foreign Policy, 1918–45*, Series D (1937–45), Vol. I, p. 69 f.

Britain, only the methods employed by Hitler to achieve his ends. Still, no action was taken to warn Hitler in no uncertain terms to desist from any future act of this type. France was held in line, and no definite British statement was made that Britain would assist France in the case of a German attack on Czechoslovakia.* The Soviet Union, alarmed by the German expansion toward southeastern Europe, proposed to Britain on March 18 a four power conference to discuss means of preventing further aggression, but the proposal was rejected by the Chamberlain cabinet and publicly called by the Prime Minister a method of dividing Europe into two opposing camps and a sure way of plunging Britain into war. In May, 1938, rumors were rife that Germany was set for an attack on Czechoslovakia. At that moment France and Russia declared their willingness to stand by their Czechoslovak ally, and Britain made it clear that she could not be expected to be a disinterested onlooker. As a consequence, Germany hastily withdrew, though Hitler was confident that the unity of the three powers could be broken up in the end.

Hitler was right in this belief. Chamberlain had made up his mind that the "great coalition" proposed by Winston Churchill was unfeasible, since Russia was weak.† In addition, he argued that even by the concerted action of the three powers Czechoslovakia could not be saved from German invasion and destruction. The Chief-of-Staff of the German army, General Ludwig Beck, probably the best brain in the German army, took a very different view of the situation. He was firmly convinced that Germany could not hope to win a war against Czechoslovakia if France and Britain intervened.‡ Beck was reasonably certain that the German army could break the Czech fortifications after

---

* Cf. Wheeler-Bennett: *Munich, Prologue to Tragedy*, pp. 34 ff.

† See K. Feiling: *The Life of Neville Chamberlain* (London: 1946), p. 403. Also Churchill's chapters on Munich in his *The Second World War: The Gathering Storm*, Vol. I, pp. 277–321.

‡ His memoranda of this period have appeared in W. Foerster: *Ein General kämpft gegen den Krieg* (Munich: 1949).

sixteen days of fighting, but he felt that the defeat of Czechoslovakia would mean as little as the defeat of Serbia had meant in World War I. His feelings were so strong that he was willing to lead the army in a revolt against the National Socialist regime if Hitler brought on a war in which Britain and France took part. The preparations for such a *coup d'état* were made circumspectly, and the British Government was informed of the existence of the movement.*

One can query whether the British Government ever paid any attention to the internal conflicts of Germany. Unaccustomed to totalitarian conditions the vast majority of the British public took the genuine enthusiasm of the mass of the German people as a plebiscite in favor of Hitler. It seemed unrealistic to deal with conspirators, because history was made by nations and their governments. British foreign policy had travelled a long way from the days of Canning and Palmerston, when Britain felt no compunction about supporting revolts and revolutions, provided they aimed in the right direction. Irrespective of what had already happened, Neville Chamberlain decided to find a solution to the European tension by direct negotiation with Hitler and Mussolini, even if this approach meant an unprecedented connivance at the designs of the dictators.

The Treaty of Munich of September 29, 1938, which gave Hitler the Sudetenland, was the result of Chamberlain's exertions for achieving a multilateral settlement with Nazi Germany. It was brought about by bringing the utmost Anglo-French pressure to bear upon the Czechoslovak Government. France most flagrantly violated her treaties with allied Czechoslovakia. The Czechs had not even a voice in the drafting of the Munich Treaty. Both Britain and France also disregarded their obligations under the League Covenant and refused co-operation with the other great power, Russia, which had become a member of the League Council. All was done in the expectation that the

* H. Rothfels: *The German Opposition to Hitler* (Hinsdale, Ill.: 1948), pp. 58–63.

full realization of the principle of nationality would afford a better foundation of the European peace and that Nazi Germany, once her grievances against Versailles were stilled, would become a law-abiding member of the European community. Both these hopes proved almost immediately highly dubious. The concessions made by Hitler in his negotiations with Chamberlain in September, 1938, were small compared to his gains. He had threatened to march into Czechoslovakia on October 1, and this he did, though the German army, thanks to British diplomacy, did not have to fire a shot. In return Hitler had to limit his demands for annexation of the Sudetenland to clearly German regions. An international commission, composed of representatives of Britain, France, Germany, Italy, and Czechoslovakia, was to draw the final frontiers arranging for a plebiscite in controversial regions.

No plebiscite was ever held. The work of the international commission proved a sham. Germany dictated the terms of the final settlement. Britain and France had to submit to German demands if they were not to announce to the world a few weeks after Munich that there was no "peace in our time." The final settlement of November 21, 1938, gave Germany 2.8 million Sudeten Germans and 0.8 million Czechs. It was carefully drafted so as to leave rump-Czechoslovakia entirely defenseless, and the quarter million Germans left there were an element of subversion that the Nazi Government could use at will.* The settlement made Hitler's march into Prague in March, 1939, an easy stroll.

The Munich Treaty gave Germany undisputed control over southeastern Europe on the condition that Hitler would not go to war and would respect certain rules of international law. If Hitler had been satisfied with the annexation of Austria and Sudetenland, he could have gained ever increasing control over southeastern Europe through peaceful economic and political penetration. It was unlikely

* Cf. Wheeler-Bennett: *Munich, Prologue to Tragedy*, pp. 175 ff., 192 ff.

that the western European powers would have had either the mind or the means to challenge such a German policy, which could have led to a German-dominated federation of *Mitteleuropa*. Undoubtedly, Poland under these circumstances would have had no other choice but to agree to modifications of the status of Danzig and the Corridor. In fact, she was ready to make concessions even in 1939. On the other hand, Russia would have grown uneasy over an eastward expansion of Germany, but she could hardly have interfered without the active support of the western European powers. Actually, as seen from the Kremlin, Britain and France, in excluding the Soviet Union from the Munich settlement, had turned the pressure of German power deliberately away from western Europe toward Russia.

Yet it is idle to speculate on the course that history might have taken if Hitler had concentrated on the peaceful exploitation of his vast gains after 1938. He had geared the German economy to war and prepared the German people for tribal conquest. Indeed, he had been pouting already when Chamberlain at Munich deprived him of "his" war. Thus the march into Prague, and almost immediately thereafter, the struggle for Poland followed. Munich cannot be defended on any good ground. It is true that the British people were ready to face the worst in the fall of 1939, whereas in 1938 they had been dreaming about a good world; but French morale did not visibly improve during the year. The Molotov-Ribbentrop Pact of August 23, 1939, and the Communist opposition to the "imperialist war" added to the internal French dissensions. It has been argued that Chamberlain was buying time for the rearmament of Britain by concluding the Munich Treaty,* but the western powers lost from thirty-five to forty Czech divisions together with the Czech fortifications, which betrayed to the Germans many secrets of the Maginot line. The industrial capacity of Czechoslovakia, includ-

* K. Feiling: *The Life of Neville Chamberlain* (London: 1946), pp. 381 ff.

ing the big Skoda works, augmented the German armaments drive, which proceeded at a faster pace than that of
the western powers. Churchill's estimate that German military strength almost doubled during 1938–9 is no exag-
geration.*

In the light of history, Munich appears as one of the
great turning points of world history. The western European powers voluntarily surrendered their influence over
eastern Europe, and they failed to regain it in World
War II in spite of American participation. The year 1938
was also the last in which the western European powers
could have co-operated with the Soviet Union without paying a heavy price for her assistance. After Munich the future of Europe east of the Rhine and, indeed, as the
events of 1939–40 were to show, of the whole Continent
rested with Hitler and Stalin. Out of the wreckage of the
European state system, American participation in World
War II helped to salvage only western Europe and the
larger part of Germany and Austria.

In spite of many disappointments that Hitler caused the
western European powers after Munich, Neville Chamberlain clung to the hope that he had brought stability to
Europe with an almost religious fervor. The news of
Hitler's march into Prague did not seriously shake his
faith, and his statements in Parliament on March 15–16,
1939 indicated that he would have condoned Hitler's new
breach of faith. The British nation, however, became
alarmed at seeing the Germans tear up treaties and expose
Britain as unable to make good her guarantee of new
Czech frontiers. Lord Halifax persuaded the Prime Minister, as he had finally persuaded himself, that whatever the
risk, Britain had to resist any further rampage of Hitler.†
British diplomats suddenly realized that the Vistula was as
important as the Rhine, but their attempt in 1939 at building up an eastern "cordon" against Germany with Ru-

* Churchill: *The Second World War: The Gathering Storm,*
Vol. I, pp. 336 ff.
† Wheeler-Bennett: *Munich, Prologue to Tragedy,* pp. 349 ff.

mania, Hungary, and Poland was more an act of faith than a political performance. In any event, the decisive question was the future attitude of the Soviet Union, and this diplomatic problem was tackled last.

In the summer of 1939 it became clear that effective military co-operation between Russia and the new Anglo-French entente would be even more difficult than it had been during World War I. The Russians undoubtedly knew that the western European powers had decided, at least for the initial phase of the imminent war, upon a defensive strategy in the west,* and that the Russians thus would have to carry the burden of the fight. It was possible that the western European armies would not go beyond what came to be known as a *Sitzkrieg* and that Chamberlain might conclude a new compromise at the expense of Russia. It is at least understandable that the Soviet Government entertained grave suspicions in view both of the events prior to 1939 and of the realities of the moment.

The Soviet rulers were asked to assume awful risks when they were invited to join in the resistance against Hitler.† Under these circumstances it was logical that they requested permission to occupy the natural ramparts in the Baltic that had protected Russia in the eighteenth and nineteenth centuries and that they inquired whether Russian troops could move through Poland and Rumania. The answers were disappointing. Poland refused to admit Russian troops and generally resented the idea of a military pact between the western European nations and the Soviet Union. The Molotov-Ribbentrop Pact of August 23, 1939, was the result of this unexampled breakdown of every con-

---

* In May, 1939 during Franco-Polish staff conversations, General Gamelin indicated that France would open an offensive against Germany with 35–38 divisions on the sixteenth day after mobilization. This statement, however, was later declared not to have been a binding promise. Cf. L. B. Namier: *Diplomatic Prelude* (London: 1948), pp. 456–66.

† Cf. L. B. Namier's article "The Anglo-French-Russian Negotiations of 1939" in his *Europe in Decay*, pp. 238–58.

certed action. Under the terms of the treaty the Soviet Union could occupy most of the Baltic states, Bessarabia, and one third of Poland. Ribbentrop had even been authorized by Hitler to write into the pact Germany's political disinterestedness in southeastern Europe and to include, if the Russians insisted, the Turkish Straits and Turkey; but Molotov did not raise these demands.* Russia's western defenses were greatly improved and, for the time being at least, Russia was relieved of the threat of a German attack. Germany was turned against western Europe.

It would be difficult to find in international history a comparable moment of general confusion. Every major actor in the events of 1939 was sooner or later to discover his lack of foresight. The final result of the war should have convinced the Germans of the criminal folly committed by Hitler not only in unleashing a general war but also in removing the buffers between Russia and Germany that had largely been created by German military efforts in World War I. The blind contempt that the Germans had always felt for the Poles played an important part in these events.

Stalin himself soon had reason to rethink the practicability of the Soviet-German Pact. The consequences of this eastern "Munich" were as catastrophic as those of the Munich treaty of 1938. The pact was concluded in the hope that a struggle between Germany and the western European Powers would ensue and that it would last some time and weaken Germany as well. Stalin's general judgment—that France and Britain were weak, although Germany was inclined to underrate British skill and determination†—proved correct, but the Nazi conquest of the Continent was even faster and more thorough than the Russian leaders had expected. There is a bitter note in all

---

* R. J. Sontag and J. S. Beddie (eds.): *Nazi-Soviet Relations 1939–1941* (Washington, D.C.: 1948), pp. 157 f.
† *Nazi-Soviet Relations, 1939–1941*, p. 74.

subsequent reported statements by Stalin on France; he felt
that she had "opened the gates to the fascist enemy," contributed less to the final victory than the Poles, and should
not be readmitted to the councils of the great powers.*
Once Russia was attacked by Hitler's armies in 1941, the
Soviet Union realized the need for co-operation with western Europe and began to clamor for the "second front"
that she herself had helped to undermine by her assistance
to Hitler and the propaganda of the Comintern, which had
been particularly effective in France.

But it should not be overlooked that Russia, even at the
height of German power in the fall and winter of 1940,
did not give up certain interests, even across the line of
demarcation that the pact of 1939 seemed to have drawn
between Germany and Russia. In his talks with Hitler
and Ribbentrop in November, 1940, Molotov firmly insisted upon Russia's right to the Turkish Straits and adjacent Balkan areas.† He was not cajoled by Ribbentrop
into accepting an outlet to the Persian Gulf instead. Nor
was Molotov impressed by Ribbentrop's glib sales talk
about the defeat of England, which the German minister
asserted had actually already been accomplished. Molotov's
shrewd and cagey statements in Berlin were an indication that the Russians derived some comfort and courage
from Britain's continued resistance after the battle of
France and western Europe had been lost. On the basis of
the available documents no one can say whether Molotov
and other Russian leaders considered in this connection the
interest that the United States took in the independence of
the British Isles and of the British Commonwealth; but
we may surmise that the expressions of American sentiment and official policy were carefully analyzed in the
Kremlin.

* J. F. Byrnes: *Speaking Frankly* (New York: 1947), pp. 25, 28.
† *Nazi-Soviet Relations, 1939–1941*, pp. 217–54. Cf. M. Beloff:
The Foreign Policy of Soviet Russia (London: 1949), Vol. II, pp.
349 ff

2. THE GREAT ALLIANCE

THE Continent was soon virtually in Hitler's hands. Poland was quickly defeated in September, 1939, and
western Europe was overrun in the summer of 1940. Before long these conquests were rounded off with the occupation of southeastern Europe and the Balkans as far
south as Crete. The defeated nations were deeply shaken in
their traditional beliefs, and if Hitler had offered them a
dignified role in a reorganized Europe, he might have
been able to consolidate his conquests and might even have
received considerable support for his war against Russia.
However, his "new order" of Europe was only a device for
the rule of a master race over subjugated peoples, and
Hitler's "crusade" to protect European civilization against
the Russian menace was an equally false label. Inevitably, resistance to German military government grew, particularly after the German war machine stalled in Russia
and the Allies could begin to extend active support to the
national undergrounds.

Nevertheless, the defeated nations of the European Continent ceased after 1940–1 to be a major element in de-
ciding the fate of Europe, and the circumstances of their
defeat and their subsequent Nazi bondage made it extremely doubtful that they could easily recover something
approximating their former political stature after liberation. As in the years after 1809, only Russia and Britain
seemed to count, but the differences in the historical ages
were great. Napoleon's European regime did not have the
methods of the twentieth-century police-state at its disposal nor the planned war economy in which millions of
vanquished people could be exploited for the industrial production of the victorious state. Early nineteenth-century
warfare and resistance depended on arms that could be
supplied with relatively small effort, while in the modern
age highly technical weapons were required. The speedy

rearming of Prussia after 1812, largely accomplished with British assistance, could not be repeated with France or Belgium in 1944.

There were other differences between the early nineteenth and the twentieth centuries. In 1810 Britain fought her continental wars with small armies augmented by allied and auxiliary European forces. During World War I, however, she was compelled to mobilize a large national-service army, and even then she achieved only a stabilization of the western front in France; without American assistance the western European powers could not have turned the balance against Germany in 1918, particularly in view of the breakdown of czarist Russia. The battle of France in 1940 left Britain without any continental allies, and an invasion of the Continent by the British and British Commonwealth forces after 1940 could not have broken Hitler's iron grip on the Continent. Even the mere defense of the British Isles and the empire required at least the financial and industrial support of the United States.

Hitler's invasion of Russia in June, 1941, and his declaration of war on the United States after Pearl Harbor made it possible to plan realistically the full destruction of the Nazi domination of Europe. Without the gallant and prodigious war effort of Britain, American power could never have been brought to bear upon Germany, as Americans well knew. Incidentally, even the Russians should ponder what might have happened to them if the British had not fought on after Dunkirk. Nevertheless, from 1941 until 1944 the Russians had to carry the main burden of the German war, with losses of life and devastation of land such as no people has suffered in modern history. They cannot claim that they won the war by themselves, but it is correct to say that they broke the *offensive* power of the German army, particularly in the gigantic struggle on the plains of southern Russia during the winter of 1942–3. The isolation of the Sixth Army around Stalingrad took place at the same time that Anglo-American forces landed in north Africa. After the fall of Stalingrad the Russians began their advances to the west, tying down the bulk of the German armies in the process, and deflecting to the east most of Germany's war production, which continued to rise until early 1944.

Undoubtedly, American and British lend-lease deliveries contributed to the Russian successes, but how much it is impossible to say.* The official Russian contention today is that they constituted four per cent of the Russian war production, probably too low a figure. Moreover, at the critical turning point of the war, before the transplanted Russian factories were fully operating, even a smaller percentage of the over-all production, if delivered in time, could have been decisive. On the other hand, could the Western powers have afforded to see the Soviet Union knocked out? The Russians, for their part, did not complain so much about Western niggardliness with regard to lend-lease as they did about the lack of a second front, which seemed to indicate a hesitation on the part of the Western powers to commit their major military forces to an invasion of the Continent. The United Nations Declaration of January 1, 1942, pledged all signatories to support each other by employing their "full resources, military or economic, against those members of the Tripartite Pact and its adherents with which such government is at war." † But until June, 1944 the Western Allies could not use their full military resources.

A good case can be made out to prove that a cross-channel operation in 1942 or early 1943 would have brought little relief to the Russians. General Marshall urged such an operation in the event that the Russian front should be seriously disrupted by the Germans,‡ but he was overruled

* Even the chief of the American military mission to Russia, General Deane, does not arrive at a clear answer. J. R. Deane: *The Strange Alliance* (New York: 1947). Cf. his statements p. 87 and 95.

† L. M. Goodrich (ed.): *Documents on American Foreign Relations* (Boston: 1942), Vol. IV, p. 203.

‡ Cf. H. L. Stimson and McG. Bundy: *On Active Service in Peace and War* (New York: 1948), pp. 560 ff. Cf. also General Mar-

in the combined Anglo-American councils, and Churchill's strategy of limited investments and peripheral approaches prevailed for the time being. The Anglo-American armies invaded north Africa and Sicily and proceeded to assault the Italian peninsula. Only thereafter did General Marshall's conception of a massed invasion of northwestern Europe become the central theme of Western strategy. Nevertheless, Churchill was always convinced that only a Western offensive aiming at the liberation of France and the Lowlands together with a Western invasion of Germany could decide the war. He differed with American strategic planners mainly in his judgment as to a feasible date for a cross-channel invasion of Europe. He was rightly convinced that such a formidable enterprise needed time for the amassing of sufficiently large and fully trained forces as well as for the construction of amphibious craft—to mention only the most important needs. His judgment that the cross-channel invasion would be possible at best in 1943 was proven correct. In the absence of an adequate number of landing craft, which necessitated a postponement of the Operation Overlord till the early summer of 1944, the Prime Minister's urgent advice to have the Anglo-American armies cross from Sicily into Italy was very sound.

It would have made a very bad impression if the Western Allies had not used their forces to engage the enemy in combat while the Russians were fighting Germany over a thousand mile front in deadly battle.* The Italian theater, of course, could not be the scene of the major decisions of the war. The number of divisions that Hitler was forced to invest in Italy was not much greater than the number used by the Allies, and the attrition of the German army during the campaign, though by no means negligible, could not tip the scale of the general war. Still,

shall's report *The Winning of the War in Europe and the Pacific* (Washington, D.C.: 1945), pp. 8 ff.; D. D. Eisenhower: *Crusade in Europe* (Garden City, N.Y.: 1948), pp. 44 ff., 66 ff., 138 f., 167.

* W. S. Churchill: *The Second World War: The Hinge of Fate,* Vol. IV, (Boston: 1950) pp. 790 ff.

the political gains were considerable. The breakdown of
Mussolini's regime had a great effect on anti-Hitler resistance all over Europe. Though the Western Allies failed
to capture all of Italy, or even Rome, in the days following
the Badoglio revolt and the armistice, Mussolini was
reduced to a mere puppet of Hitler.

Winston Churchill was much preoccupied with safeguard-
ing the future of the Balkans and of southeastern Europe.
He would have liked to start a Balkan front, but he seems
to have understood quite clearly that Turkey had first to
be persuaded to enter the war.* However, the idea of a
Balkan front to be launched by Turkey with the assistance
of the Allies proved impracticable. In the first place, the
Turks refused to co-operate. They knew quite well that
Russia was most emphatically interested in gaining control
of Bulgaria and in revising the Turkish Straits regime as
established by the Montreux Convention of 1936; and an
expansion of Turkey's influence in the Balkans would have
strained future Turkish relations with a victorious Russia,
while during 1941–4 Istanbul and Ankara were within
the easy range of German bombing planes. Furthermore if
Turkey had entered the war, she would have required an
amount of Allied support that would have seriously interfered with the execution of the invasion of France.

Some apprehension on the part of the American Joint
Chiefs-of-Staff was engendered by Churchill's suggestion.
They became very sensitive when Churchill, even after
the Turkish refusal to co-operate, proposed secondary operations such as an invasion of Rhodes or diversionary moves
to support Tito, whom, under British prodding, the United
States had accepted as the leader of Yugoslav resistance.
This irritation was understandable, though the black suspicions about British unwillingness to fight that this and
similar episodes aroused in the rigid soul of Admiral Leahy,
were far off the mark.†

---

* Churchill: *The Second World War: The Hinge of Fate*, Vol.
IV, p. 791.
   † W. D. Leahy: *I Was There* (New York: 1950), pp. 238, 242

The general strategy that the American Chiefs-of-Staff had devised under General Marshall's leadership was essentially right. It was based on Clausewitz's dictum that the supreme strategic aim must be the annihilation of the enemy's army and that such an end can be attained only by the use of the maximum of the available forces. The Balkan peninsula, or, for that matter, even Italy, constituted the hard shell rather than the "soft underbelly" of the European Continent. Partly because of the nature of the countries involved, partly because of supply lines much longer than those required for a cross-channel operation, only a part of the Anglo-American forces could have been used and only relatively small German forces could have been brought to bay in the Mediterranean. The northwestern European theater was the single battleground where the western powers could deploy the mass of their armed divisions backed by their naval and air superiority. Here they could use their armed strength most effectively in a war of maneuver likely to lead eventually to the capture of the main arsenal of the enemy, the Ruhr. But even this strategy depended heavily on military co-operation with Russia, since it could attain its supreme objectives only if the Red army continued to hold down the bulk of the German forces.

After Pearl Harbor the problem of Russian military co-operation loomed larger in the minds of American military and political planners than did political considerations. "Let us win the war first and talk about politics thereafter" became the oft-heard political slogan. The situation of the United States and her allies in 1942 was extremely perilous, and as long as the mere survival of the independent nations was in doubt, political warfare had to aim almost exclusively at the support of pending military operations. Nevertheless, war itself is an act of policy by which one power wants to impose its will upon another in order to check a threat to its own existence or to a peaceful international order. Obviously no state has ever won a peace of its liking by losing a war, but soldiers will fight a futile war if its political implications are not clearly faced. War will inevitably affect the power relationship among states, even allied states, and without the establishment of a new balance of power no international order can be built, particularly if the major nations are ideologically divided.

The relationship between the politics of war and those of peace were never fully grasped either by the military or by the civilian heads of the American government, for they were not, like Churchill, accustomed to imperial and global thinking by former experiences. The Joint Chiefs-of-Staff were convinced that the Axis powers could be defeated at a reasonably early date only if Russia could be kept in the war. Their military opinion carried great weight with President Roosevelt, who after Pearl Harbor gave his duties as commander-in-chief highest priority. If the Western powers wanted to achieve a maximum of co-operation with the Soviet Union, so it was argued, all unnecessary political questions that might flare up into embarrassing conflicts should be avoided; otherwise the Soviet Union might possibly be driven to conclude a separate peace.

The problem of whether or not Stalin and Hitler could have made a separate peace after 1941 cannot be settled, since nobody can document the Russian side of the story. The captured German documents, however, contain no proof that Hitler ever contemplated any deal with Stalin after 1941; and Stalin, while in retreat before Hitler's cohorts in 1941 and 1942, could not have made an agreement with Hitler, because the Soviet regime would have broken down. After Stalingrad all indications were that Stalin was determined to go through with the full annihilation of Nazi Germany and to secure Russia's western frontier, where she had been invaded in 1812, 1914, and 1941, each time suffering grievous losses. There were signs that Stalin instead feared negotiations between Germany and the Western powers, and the Free German Committee that he created in Moscow in 1943 was an instrument of psychological warfare against the western Allies as much as against the Germans.*

It is possible, therefore, that Anglo-American policy vis-à-vis the Soviet Union could have been somewhat more courageous in exploring Russian postwar intentions and the possibilities of preliminary agreements on basic questions of a new political order. Before Pearl Harbor the Soviet Union demanded from Britain as the basis of such discussion the recognition of the Russian frontiers of 1941—that is, of Russia's annexation of the Baltic republics, eastern Poland, Bessarabia, and Bucovina. The American Government urged the British cabinet most strongly not to commit itself to any specific postwar arrangements that might undermine confidence in the Atlantic Charter. All such specific settlements were to wait for a general peace conference.† This same point of view, which was forcefully advocated by Cordell Hull, was retained after the United States had entered the war. The Russians thereafter did not urge inter-Allied conversations on political problems of the future peace, but once their armies returned to eastern Europe they began to act in an alarming fashion by organizing it according to their own wishes.

Official American policy saw in the Atlantic Charter the program of the United Nations. As Sumner Welles has remarked, however, the Charter provided a highly desirable pattern, but a pattern that could only assume meaning according to its actual application to concrete issues.‡ An attempt to find a common policy for the three big powers would have had a greater chance of success if it had been undertaken at a time when the vast military strength of the Soviet Union was not yet fully revealed. Instead,

* Cf. E. H. Boehm: " 'Free Germans' in Soviet Psychological Warfare," *Public Opinion Quarterly*, (1950), Vol. XIV pp. 285–95.

† C. Hull: *Memoirs* (New York: 1948), Vol. II, pp. 1165 ff. Cf. also S. Welles: "Two Roosevelt Decisions: One Debit, One Credit," *Foreign Affairs* (1951), Vol. XXIX, pp. 182–204.

‡ Welles: "Two Roosevelt Decisions", p. 183.

American foreign policy concentrated on the building of a permanent United Nations organization, a highly commendable aim, but one that left out the settlement of the immediate issues that the war had raised.* The United Nations Charter expressly reserves the right to draft the peace treaties with the former Axis states to the belligerent nations.

Actually the United States was forced after 1943 to negotiate with the Soviet Union on some concrete issues, but they were always discussed piecemeal and not in an overall review of the general conditions of a future peace. The first meeting of the three foreign ministers, which took place in Moscow in October, 1943, centered largely around the questions that had arisen in connection with the Anglo-American invasion of Italy, the first Allied occupation of a substantial part of an Axis country. It led to an agreement on the general organization of control in conquered or liberated countries. The declaration charged the national army commanders with the full responsibility for administering military government, though some tripartite diplomatic liaison was created. The agreement on the organization of military government proved more important than principles proposed for regulating the conduct of Allied military government in all areas. The democratic aims stated in the Moscow Declaration left too many loopholes for an unscrupulous Russian interpretation. Rumania, Bulgaria, and Hungary, all of which came under Russian occupation, were almost immediately set on the road toward a Russian-style "people's democracy."

The Moscow Conference of October, 1943 also produced a joint tripartite declaration on the intended restoration of Austria. This was the first specific and positive Allied peace

* Certain U. S. government offices prepared extensive studies. With the exception of the work done in preparation of the United Nations Charter few of these studies exercised a marked influence upon high policy. See Hull: *Memoirs*, Vol. II, pp. 1626–55. Also *Postwar Foreign Policy Preparation, 1939–1945*, Department of State Publication 3580 (Washington, D.C.: 1949).

aim affecting the future disposition of the territories of Greater Germany. The postwar treatment of Germany, too, was informally discussed by the three foreign ministers in Moscow and a month later by the Big Three at Teheran.

The German question faced by the Allied statesmen can be divided into three parts in relation first to Allied political warfare, second to the post-hostilities period, third to the final peace settlement. Much criticism has recently been levelled against President Roosevelt for his proclamation of "unconditional surrender" of the Axis states as the immediate war aim of the United Nations at the close of the Casablanca Conference in January, 1943.* By this announcement, so the main argument runs, the war was prolonged unnecessarily, because the peoples of the Axis states were induced to fight with greater determination and reject ideas of revolt.† However, the conception that totalitarian governments can be wrecked by popular uprisings shows a misapprehension of the modern totalitarian state. Only a split within the leadership or the defection of groups that can command the loyalty of substantial sections of the army, police, and bureaucracy can lead to a change of government. Such a *coup d'état* involves immeasurable risks and is not likely to be undertaken by patriotic men unless the very existence of their nation is at stake. In Italy the survival of the monarchy under fascism gave the anti-Mussolini revolt a legal character. In Germany all the legal bridges had been burned, and nothing but conspiracy and assassination were left as possible means for the overthrow of the Hitler regime. Only an impending national catastrophe could justify such action before the conscience of the conspirators or in the eyes of the army on which they would have to rely even if their plot should weaken the army's resistance against the enemy.

* See Churchill: *The Second World War: The Hinge of Fate,* Vol. IV, pp. 684–91. Also E. Roosevelt: *As He Saw It* (New York: 1946), p. 117 and Sherwood: *Roosevelt and Hopkins,* p. 686.
† See for example H. W. Baldwin: *Great Mistakes of the War* (New York: 1949), pp. 22–5.

The members of the Beck-Goerdeler conspiracy were almost without exception men of high, and some of them of the highest, character. They had read the writing on the wall in 1938 and had been willing to act when Chamberlain's flight to Munich frustrated their plans. The Stalingrad disaster, the approaching landings of the Allied armies, and the growing resistance in German-occupied Europe created the favorable setting for their attempt to seize power. But they failed; their bomb did not kill Hitler.

The demand for the unconditional surrender as such did not have any immediate appreciable effect upon the continuation of German armed resistance, and Stalin at Teheran in November, 1943 criticized it as being too vague and therefore apt to drive the Germans to support the existing government. It was better, he opined, to give people a clear idea about the future, even though it might at first appear to them terrifying.* Perhaps Stalin was right up to a point. If the Germans, however, had heard that the Big Three at Teheran had discussed the dismemberment of Germany as the desirable basis of a European peace, unconditional surrender would have assumed an even more ominous ring in German ears. Churchill, nowadays under fire for his assent to the unconditional surrender demand, has stressed this point in a sober appraisal of these events.† Indeed, one can hardly judge that any Soviet political warfare yielded any worthwhile results. Originally it tried to arouse the resistance of the German workers against Hitler's "imperialist" war, but there were too few German Communists left after eight years of Nazi rule to spread the new Comintern doctrine. The latter presented a radical reversal of the earlier line, which had denounced the western powers as waging an imperialist war against Hitler.‡ After Stalingrad some of the captured German of-

---

* Sherwood: *Roosevelt and Hopkins*, p. 782 f.

† Churchill: *The Second World War: The Hinge of Fate*, Vol. IV, p. 689.

‡ For the effect of this policy on the German Communist party see O. K. Flechtheim: *Die Kommunistische Partei Deutschlands in der Weimarer Republik* (Offenbach: 1948), pp. 227–9.

ficers were used to issue appeals to the German officer corps to save Germany from destruction by turning against Hitler. However, the *putsch* of July, 1944, was not east-oriented.

Allied political warfare against Germany proved exceedingly weak in these circumstances. It remained to be seen whether more effective Allied policies with regard to the post-hostilities period could be formulated. Agreement was reached at the Moscow Conference that unconditional surrender in a literal sense would apply to Germany. And although in Italy this policy had already been given an interpretation that made the word "unconditional" appear perfunctory and in Bulgaria, Rumania, and Hungary, and also in Japan it was diluted again, it was strictly enforced against Germany. Whether there would have been modifications if the Beck-Goerdeler plot had been successful must be a matter of speculation. Unconditional surrender implied the assumption of supreme executive, legislative, and judiciary functions in Germany by the conquering powers— that is, the total occupation of Germany. It would not have excluded the appointment of a temporary federal German government working under the direction and supervision of the supreme Allied authority, to be replaced in due course by a democratically elected German government.* But a clarification of this point obviously depended largely upon whether the Allies wanted a Germany or a group of German states. If they favored partition, it was useless to have any German government in the post-hostilities period.

The American delegation at the Moscow Conference proposed the establishment of a tripartite commission to draft a German surrender document and an agreement on the organization of Allied military government over Germany. The so-called European Advisory Commission, composed of

* This policy was adopted in Austria, which was to be treated as a "liberated" country, but it did not stave off the impact of the East-West split after the war. Cf. for the early period of Allied Military Government in Austria the author's report *American Military Government: Its Organization and Policies* (Washington, D.C.: 1947), pp. 75–86.

the representatives of the three powers, joined by France after her liberation, drafted these two documents after endless bargaining and haggling. The most easily concluded agreement, prepared by a decision already taken in Teheran, was the demarcation of the Soviet zone of occupation, which gave the Russians not only all of eastern but most of central Germany, thus bringing Russian armies to within less than a hundred miles of the Rhine. The Russians were offered so much chiefly because the western statesmen felt that the Soviet Union was entitled to the occupation of a third of Germany. In view of the contemplated cession of some eastern German territories to Poland and the smaller population and industries in the eastern provinces of Germany, Russia was able to claim even more than a third of the German area as her occupation zone. In the spring of 1944, when these decisions were being prepared, neither the British nor the American military leaders were optimistic in their expectations about the eastern goals that the Anglo-American forces would be able to reach after the landing in France.

However, the European Advisory Commission* envisaged the various zones as serving only as areas of military occupation and hoped that the Allied Control Council of Germany, composed of the three, later four, Allied commanders, would co-ordinate the policies in all the zones. But the Commission was never allowed to discuss the substance of what could constitute such a common Allied policy in Germany after the end of hostilities.

Russia was unwilling to commit herself to definite post-surrender and even less to final peace policies, but so were Britain and the United States. The idea of the dismemberment of Germany bedevilled the thinking of the three powers all through the war. It is interesting to note that the three foreign ministers at the Moscow Conference ad-

* Cf. the revealing articles by P. E. Mosely: "Dismemberment of Germany" and "The Occupation of Germany: New Light on How the Zones Were Drawn," *Foreign Affairs* (1950), Vol. XXVIII, pp. 487–98; pp. 580–604.

mitted to each other that their heads of government were in favor of dismemberment, whereas the best advice of their experts was against such a course.* The record of the conversations of the Big Three on German problems makes painful reading. Even if one were to approve for a moment the suggested policies, the proposals for implementing them showed that they were not built on familiarity with German history and German conditions. Roosevelt was particularly attracted by the idea of an ultimate partition of Germany, though he was at heart less strongly opposed to German economic than to German political unity, whereas the State Department under Cordell Hull was against any tampering with German unity. It was Roosevelt who brought the question of dismemberment to the fore again at the Yalta Conference in February, 1945. No decisions in this respect were taken at Yalta, but new negotiations continued in London into May, 1945. Stalin settled the issue in peremptory manner by his public declaration of May 8, 1945, that Russia did not intend "to dismember or destroy Germany." † Considering, however, that the Soviet Union had already annexed the northern part of East Prussia and was in the process of turning over all German provinces east of the Oder-Neisse line to Polish administration, the announcement sounded rather brazen; indeed, less than a year later the Soviet Union began openly to depart from every agreed Allied policy in Germany and thereby promoted a new partition.

The unsettled nature of American policy with regard to eastern and central Europe derived largely from the military needs for co-operation with the Soviet Union. It stemmed also from the lack of a sure grasp of European political conditions, which was understandable, though not necessarily excusable, considering the long aloofness of the United States from Europe. Still, American statesmen cannot be judged by their own insight without a consideration

* Mosely: "Dismemberment of Germany", p. 489. Cf. Hull: *Memoirs*, Vol. II, pp. 1284–8.
† Mosely: "Dismemberment of Germany", p. 498.

of the popular American sentiment with which they had to deal. Would the intervention of the United States in Europe again be as temporary as it had been after 1917? Very grave doubts existed about the willingness of the American people to assume long-range commitments in Europe. It was expected that America would not withdraw from a new League of Nations, and the response to the idea of a permanent United Nations Organization found in both American parties gave an early assurance that the United States would not become as isolationist a power as she had been in the interwar period. Nevertheless, special commitments in Europe beyond a participation in the Allied occupation of Germany and possibly Austria seemed outside the realm of possibility. Furthermore, with another war in the Far East still to be fought and won, once the war in Europe had come to an end, there was an imperative need for the speedy transfer of American divisions to the Pacific and a natural tendency not to be involved too deeply in European matters. Finally, there was the desire to win Russian co-operation in the war against Japan.*

Moreover, the thinking of American policy-makers was still dominated by the vague notion that somehow the old Europe would ultimately re-emerge. It was, of course, a foregone conclusion that Russia would extend her influence beyond her pre-World War II frontiers and, perhaps, even beyond her 1914 frontiers. Prussia-Germany would be wiped out as a great power, and an equivalent to the Habsburg empire in the form of a Danubian federation, for which the British hoped, was not likely to be restored. It was thought, however, that at the end of the war Britain would be able to counterbalance Russian power to some extent; she was expected to rule the Mediterranean. United States military government of Italy was, at least in its early phase, run with the idea that the British should be given every opportunity to re-establish their old economic

---

* The U.S. Army and Navy were not in agreement on the strategy for the final defeat of Japan and the need for Russian participation in the war against Japan. Cf. Leahy: *I Was There*, pp. 259, 318.

and political ties with Italy, and in Greece the American military chiefs refused to have United State troops participate in the landings. (After a great deal of argument a small group of American officers was allowed to direct the administration of civilian relief goods.) It was not foreseen that what some Americans contemptuously called British imperial interests would soon have to be taken over by the Americans in the defense of a free world.

The Italian and Greek as well as other cases made it clear that for the time being, and probably for some time to come, the United States would have to provide Britain with the means to implement her policies.* It was realized, too, that the British economy itself would have to be bolstered after the war. The prevailing opinion, however, was that Britain would get back on her feet and be capable of exercising a powerful influence in western and southern Europe. There was also the hope that France, after a more prolonged period of recuperation, would ultimately regain her prewar position, as would the Benelux and the three Scandinavian countries. The finality of the breakdown of Europe as a political system, balanced within itself, was at best sensed, but hardly recognized.

The total economic impact of the interwar period and of World War II was not fully grasped either. No doubt the American Government, backed by a substantial body of enlightened public opinion, had taken certain lessons of recent history to heart. The disastrous consequences of the treatment of reparations and war debts in the international affairs of the interwar period were not forgotten. Lend-lease avoided the pitfalls of inter-Allied financial relations that had been experienced after World War I, and in the discussion of future reparations large money payments were excluded. It was also understood that recovery had to be approached on a world-wide scale and organization.

* Sherwood: *Roosevelt and Hopkins*, prints on pp. 748 ff. a document, presumably reflecting the thinking of the Joint Chiefs-of-Staff and expressing very succinctly the opinion prevalent in this circle on the future roles of Russia and Britain in Europe.

There was general agreement, too, that it was undesirable
to have a repetition of the sudden discontinuation of the
inter-Allied economic agencies at the time of the armistice,
as had occurred in 1918 with the result that certain *ad hoc*
councils had to be improvised after a short, but costly interval. During World War II the International Monetary
Fund and the International Bank for Reconstruction and
Development were set up to act as central international
agencies in the rebuilding of world economy in the postwar era.

Nevertheless, the size of the problem involved in the reconstruction of Europe was grievously underestimated.
The United Nations Relief and Rehabilitation Administration was confined to relief operations in liberated areas during the immediate post-hostilities period. The second "R" in
U.N.R.R.A. was never pronounced. Lend-lease was brought
to an end as soon as hostilities ceased,* while the Monetary
Fund and the International Bank were given very limited means and functions. Today, when we are operating a
big civilian "lend-lease" program in the Marshall Plan,
sending military lend-lease to Turkey and Greece, and considering new projects for the North Atlantic states, one
may well wonder whether American policy could not have
achieved a much higher degree of political stability if it
could have begun to employ the financial and economic resources of the United States in a systematic plan for the
rehabilitation of Europe in 1945 instead of in 1948.

But even if the United States Government in the years
between 1943 and 1945 had diagnosed the weakness of
western Europe correctly and had been in a position to assume as onerous a role as it has taken today, it could not
have revived a European political system standing on its
own feet, as the concert of European powers had done during the nineteenth century. With the great powers in central Europe destroyed, and with western Europe weakened,

* In an interview with A. Krock (*New York Times*, February 15,
1950), President Truman has honestly admitted that the sudden termi-
nation of lend-lease was a serious error of his own policy.

there was no power in Europe that by its own strength or by alliance with all the other western European states could have blocked Russian progress into Europe. For that matter, even the United States would have been hardly strong enough to oppose the immediate demands of the Soviet Union. The decisions of the Moscow, Teheran, Yalta, and Potsdam conferences were on the whole the logical and inevitable outcome of this situation. If one wants to criticize them, one should direct criticism not so much against the actual results of the wartime conferences, which after all laid the foundations for the military defeat of the enemy countries and for the building of the United Nations, as against the expectations entertained at the time by Western statesmen with regard to the future of Western-Russian relations. The whole wartime policy of the Soviet Union, not to mention her prewar policy, demonstrated that the Soviet leaders never were ready to abandon the sovereignty of Russian policy and were determined to push Russian interests wherever they did not meet with opposition, keeping in reserve the weapons of the Communist International.

It remains a problem whether or not it would have been more practical to negotiate with Russia a clear division of spheres of interst, as the British proposed and proceeded to do in October, 1944, without much support from the American Government, which considered such spheres as incompatible with the contemplated United Nations organizations.* Under an agreement reached in Moscow in October, 1944, Rumania, Bulgaria, and Hungary were to be considered in the Russian, Greece in the British spheres of interest, while in Yugoslavia a fifty to fifty Anglo-Russian influence was to obtain. President Roosevelt gave this system his approval on a three-month "trial basis." Cordell Hull was saddened. "During the First World War," he writes, "I had made an intimate study of the system of spheres of influence and balance of power, and I was

* Hull: *Memoirs*, Vol. II, pp. 1451ff.

grounded to the taproots in their iniquitous consequences." * He was right in principle. Yet what would be
the situation of the free world today if Greece had come
under Communist control and thereby Russia had been
given free access to the Mediterranean? If the United States
had been prepared to go to war with the Soviet Union over
a direct or indirect Soviet invasion of Greece, a statement of
high principles would have sufficed; but the United States
still wanted to complete the war against Germany, Italy,
and Japan with the military co-operation of Russia, and the
American people had been told since 1941 that the Soviet
Union was on her way to become a more or less democratic state. How, under these circumstances, could anybody
stop Russia's progress into strategic areas except by direct
negotiation of spheres of military and political influence,
deplorable as this might be? Clearly, the task of statesmanship is not the mere drafting of high principles, but
the capacity for making lawful principles prevail in this
fragile human world.

Actually, the practice of the United States foreign policy
was less fastidious. The United States never considered
associating Russia with Britain and herself on equal terms
in the military government of Sicily and Italy, but this
policy inevitably meant that the Western powers would be
represented only weakly in the Soviet military government
of southeastern Europe. Czechoslovakia was informed that
she was not on the list of European states to be liberated
by Western armies. Thus Beneš had no other choice but to
conclude, on May 8, 1944, a bilateral agreement with the
Soviet Union regarding the administration of civil affairs in
Czechoslovakia after the arrival of the Russian armies.†

In such actions the Soviet Union could find her view

* Hull: *Memoirs*, Vol. II, pp. 1452 ff.
† See text in L. W. Holborn (ed.): *War and Peace Aims of the
United Nations* (Boston: 1948), Vol. II pp. 767 ff. See the exchange
of correspondence between S.H.E.A.F. and the Soviet High Com-
mand concerning Allied military operations in Czechoslovakia during
April and May, 1945, in The *New York Times*, May 10, 1948.

confirmed that western Europe would ultimately be willing to tolerate the creation of a Russian orbit along the western frontiers of the Soviet Union. And there would have been relatively little resentment in the West to such a policy if the Soviet Union had shown and maintained a minimum respect for the democratic rights and processes of the liberated eastern states. But one of the major factors that was bound to make the years between 1945 and 1947 barren years in the progress of a European peace settlement was probably the expectation of the Kremlin that, in the absence of a constructive program of stabilization for western Europe, time was on the Russian side, and that social disintegration would open new opportunities for Russian influence and perhaps give them full control over the rest of the Continent.

VII

EUROPE AND THE WORLD

AFTER THE WAR

IN May, 1945, when fighting ceased in Europe, it became evident that only two independent great powers, or superpowers,* had survived the war, the Soviet Union and the United States. The United States, Britain, the British Commonwealth, and France had less than a hundred divisions in Europe, whereas the Soviet Union had two hundred and fifty.† These figures, however, do not represent an accurate comparison of relative strength, since Russian divisions were weaker in manpower, firepower, and mobility. Moreover, the Western air forces were much greater, as were the Western navies. On the other hand, the United States fought a war three thousand miles from home, which inevitably imposed great strains on the supply services and transportation.

But it is superfluous to attempt an exact estimate of the ratio of strength between the Western and Soviet military forces in Europe, because the United States was bent upon the redeployment of her European divisions in the Pacific and when the collapse of Japan became imminent in July, 1945, the domestic political forces insisted on a speedy and radical demobilization of the American military establish-

* W. T. R. Fox: *The Super-Powers* (New York: 1944).
† A. Guillaume: *Soviet Arms and Soviet Power* (Washington, D.C.: 1949).

ment irrespective of the political consequences. Within half
a year American military power was hopelessly dilapidated.
The demand of the armed forces for universal military training was also rejected by a country that believed that the war
had been won and that to achieve the right peace settlement
was the job of diplomats, of the United Nations, and possibly some rehabilitation loans.

For a while American public sentiment seemed to veer
very close to a repetition of the attitudes after World War
I; but there was never any doubt that the United States
would maintain an active role in the United Nations and in
the occupation of Japan, Germany, Austria, and Trieste.
The support given to these operations by Congress fell
short of the actual needs, particularly in 1946–7, and
many opportunities for constructive American action were
thereby missed. The United States succeeded, however, in
holding the lines in Europe behind which the United States
token forces were stationed, although Poland and all of
eastern Europe came under the complete influence of the
Kremlin.

The absorption of eastern Europe was primarily the result of Soviet imperialism, and in each country, including
Czechoslovakia, the presence or the direct threat of the
Red army proved the determining factor of Soviet success.
Thus the only country that reasserted its national auton-
omy, even though Communist, was Yugoslavia, which had
not been liberated nor conquered directly by the Soviet
army. One should not, however, forget entirely the history
of the relations between the Western powers and these
countries in the interwar period and during World War II.
Leaving out Czechoslovakia, which, in spite of her internal nationality problems, became a democratic state, all
the eastern European states proved incapable of solving
their social, economic, and constitutional problems,* and
Czechoslovakia was abandoned to Hitler in 1938. In 1939,
Britain and France failed to give the slightest military sup-

* Cf. Hugh Seton-Watson: *Eastern Europe Between the Wars,*
1918–41 (2nd ed., London: 1946).

port to Poland, and except for some assistance to the Yugoslav partisans, the Western powers made no attempt to contribute directly to the liberation of eastern Europe from the Nazi yoke. Thus eastern Europe was opened to Russia.

It is also fair to point out that the Western Allies, though they extracted during the war certain promises from Russia concerning the establishment of democratic rights in eastern Europe, did not feel in a position to press for strong guarantees. Allied policy with regard to these regions was lukewarm during the war because of the desire for military co-operation with Russia; afterwards the concentration upon the reconversion to peacetime tasks, together with the lack of military power, prohibited Western action against the Russian absorption of the eastern European states.

However, Russia's appetite did not stop there. Stalin had insisted during the war that there should be a Polish government agreeable to the Soviet Union. Once the Russian armies had entered Poland on their march toward Berlin, he demanded the establishment of a Polish government, such as he had constituted in Lublin, that would see eye to eye with the Soviet High Command. At Yalta, Stalin had accepted some representation of the Polish Government-in-exile in London and promised democratic elections after the war; but he had also demanded the final cession of the Polish territories that he had acquired under the Molotov-Ribbentrop Pact of 1939. Since the Russo-Polish frontier of 1939 followed, broadly speaking, the proposal that Lord Curzon had made in 1921 for a just settlement of Poland's eastern boundaries, Anglo-American policy did not oppose the Soviet demand. Moreover, Britain and America indicated at an early moment that the Polish minority in the former eastern Poland should be re-settled in territories to be taken from Germany.

The Polish Government-in-exile in London had started to clamor for the annexation of all German lands east of the Oder-Neisse line, including not only East Prussia and Danzig but also the whole province of Silesia, most of Pomerania, and parts of Brandenburg. Stalin, who wished to gain support for his Lublin Committee, could do no less, though the fulfillment of these wild Polish dreams was bound to prove in part a handicap of future Russian policy in Germany. In the Anglo-Russian conversations on spheres of influence in October, 1944, the Soviet Union secured British approval of the western expansion of Poland. American diplomacy balked at the idea of uprooting millions of Germans from a country that they had inhabited for almost ten centuries. But the Americans were told at Yalta that the Germans were fleeing before the Russian armies, and it was agreed that "in due course" the Polish Government should be consulted on the extent of the western accessions, though the drawing of the final frontiers was still to be left to the peace conference.

The whole issue was thereby hopelessly compromised. The Russians turned over the administration of the German territories east of the Oder-Neisse line to the Poles as the Russian armies occupied them in their westward progress. At the Potsdam Conference in July, 1945, the Russians admitted this unilateral solution, which was in stark contrast to the discussions held by the Allied powers during the war, all of which officially envisaged an Allied occupation of the Germany of 1937.* The provisional Polish Government testified at Potsdam that only about one and a half million Germans were left in the regions that they wished to acquire; but soon thereafter the Allied Control Council for Germany had to make arrangements for the acceptance of more than five million Germans from the new German-Polish provinces.† By achieving this solution the Soviet

* That is, the Germany of 1919 plus the Saar district returned to her by the plebiscite of 1935, but shorn of all military conquests beginning with Austria in 1938.

† Together with the Germans driven out from southeastern Europe the number of German expellees was close to 10 million, the greatest migration of people in modern European history.

Union became the chief benefactor and protector of the new Poland, but also extended her potential influence into Germany. Any change of the German-Polish boundaries, which inevitably became a major desire of Germany, depended thereafter on the political goodwill of the Soviet rulers.

It has been mentioned before that no definite American policy with regard to Germany had been formulated prior to VE-day. Not only had the question of German partition proved an obstacle that American policy-makers could not overcome, but the general treatment to be meted out to the Germans remained under constant discussion without finding a clear-cut solution. Inevitably, the problem of the treatment of Germany had to be viewed in the light of future Russo-American relations, and undoubtedly the claims of the country that had suffered most from German aggression and done most to destroy German power could not be disregarded. Nor could the wishes of the other western or eastern neighbors of Germany, however vindictive, be entirely neglected. They had endured four to five years of Nazi occupation, and they were supposed to get along with Germany in Europe after the war.

The plan to make Germany, immediately after the surrender, hand over part of her industrial assets to restore the productivity of the countries crippled by her was justifiable. A large segment of German industry was geared to military production; furthermore, in 1945 not even gold could buy the industrial equipment needed for the revival of industries in Russia, Belgium, France, and other Allied countries. There was also no serious moral objection to lowering the German standard of living for some time in order to help the reconstruction of the economies of the European Allies.

However, few people in 1944–6 appreciated the narrow limitations of such a policy. Germany still was bound to remain the chief industrial country of Europe, and on her production and purchasing power the future prosperity of the Continent largely depended. It was argued that the

extermination of German industries was necessary in order
to annihilate the German potential for war, because the
disarmament provisions of the Versailles Treaty had proved
of no avail. But, though the disarmament articles of the
Versailles Treaty left many loopholes that the Germans
exploited to the utmost, their rearmament could have been
checked very easily if the victors of 1919 had continued to
act in concert and had enforced the disarmament provisions. Whether or not Germany could be kept disarmed
after World War II did not depend on the imposed de-
industrialization, but first on the possibility of keeping the
wartime alliance together and second on the ability of the
Allied powers to develop a democratic German state that
would control the aggressive forces of German society. No
democratic life could be expected to grow in Germany if
the Germans were deprived of every prospect for attaining
in years to come a decent standard of living; and with the
loss of a quarter of her territories and about ten million
Germans added to the population of rump-Germany the
need for industrial activity became even greater.

In 1944–5 such common sense did not prevail in Washington. Secretary Henry Morgenthau, Jr. could draft his
maladroit plan for the postwar treatment of Germany and
have it get serious consideration from President Roosevelt,
who took it to his conference with Churchill in Quebec in
September, 1944, where both signed it. Fortunately, President Roosevelt soon disavowed the plan, and so did the
British.* In addition to the partition of Germany this plan
proposed the full destruction of all German heavy industry.
Germany was to be allowed only an agrarian economy
and some light industries resting on an agrarian structure.
Morgenthau thought that his plan would please everybody
except the Germans. The British would like it because,
with German industries eliminated, they would be able to
inherit the world market. The Russians would see in the
plan an American attempt to conform to their "tough"

* Cf. H. Morgenthau, Jr.: *Germany is Our Problem* (New York:
1945).

ideas about the treatment of Germany. The United States could withdraw her troops quickly, since with the extirpation of the German war potential the occupation could be turned over to the European nations, the French, Czechs, Yugoslavs, Poles.

Although the author was happily unaware of such consequences, the Morgenthau plan would have been a perfect scheme for delivering Germany into the hands of the Soviet Union. The plan did not become official American policy. Cordell Hull and Henry L. Stimson prevailed upon Roosevelt to drop it, but the President then refused to make any detailed plans for the future of Germany, "a country which we do not occupy." * He tolerated only the formulation of a policy directive for the initial period of military government of Germany after the surrender, which after his death was issued by the Joint Chiefs-of-Staff to General Eisenhower. The document, known as JCS—1067, was the only American statement of postwar aims with regard to Germany, and though it was originally intended to be only an interim statement, it exercised a great influence, since most of its aims were approved by the Potsdam Conference of July, 1945.† But it should be added that the United States military government very soon softened the policies of the directive, particularly with regard to de-industrialization.

Naturally, the directors of American military government soon sensed the difficulty of withstanding the Russian pressure on Europe. In February and March, 1946, Soviet policy gave up any pretense of friendly co-operation with the Western powers. At that time the popular front policy of the Communist parties was terminated in favor of radical opposition to all bourgeois or labor governments. Simultaneously, the co-operation of the Soviet Union in the military government of Germany ceased. The Russian zone of

* Hull: *Memoirs*, Vol. II, pp. 1604–22; Stimson and Bundy: *On Active Service in Peace and War*, p. 572; Mosely: "Dismemberment of Germany", p. 491.

† Holborn: *American Military Government*, pp. 157–72, 195–205.

Germany was prepared for Sovietization.* This change of Soviet policy, which was world-wide in scope, was apparently based on a new appraisal of Western strength or weakness. The lack of military forces in western Europe and the absence of a definite plan for the rehabilitation and stabilization of the western European nations seems to have encouraged the Kremlin to anticipate a general revolutionary crisis in Europe that would enable the Soviet Union to gain complete control of the Continent. Thus about the ides of March, 1946, the cold war between the East and West began. The dividing line, running from just east of Lübeck to east of Trieste, tore asunder what was left of the largest country of Europe, Germany.

Two World Wars were fought to uphold the independence of the European nations and to maintain the free institutions on the Continent that for more than a thousand years had been the center of Western civilization, the most vigorous of all historic civilizations. But World War I had already shown that the European political system was no longer viable, but depended for its survival on the cooperation of the new overseas forces such as the United States and the dominions of the British Commonwealth. The political world system that had come into being during World War I had dissolved, it is true, after 1918, and Europe lived through the period of the twenty-years armistice in a precarious state of imbalance and division. There were free institutions in the Europe of the interwar period, but Italy soon embraced fascism, and most of the eastern European states became semi-dictatorships. In 1933, Germany chose to turn totalitarian and started to undo the peace settlement of Paris. Hitler's attack on the Soviet Union and his declaration of war against the United States made non-European powers again the arbiters of Europe's future.

The outcome of World War II proved beyond any rea-

* Cf. F. L. Neumann: "Soviet Policy in Germany," *Annals of the American Academy of Political and Social Science* (May, 1949), pp. 165–79.

sonable doubt that no western European state or, for that matter, not even all the western European nations together could resist Russia's power. To be sure, the western European states—France, Belgium, Denmark, the Netherlands, and Norway—and also Italy and Greece in the Mediterranean, as well as the major parts of Germany and Austria, were liberated by the Western forces, but only in alliance with a power profoundly opposed to democratic principles; and Russian armies had to be allowed to approach the Rhine to within less than a hundred miles. Not only is Weimar, where German humanitarian literature flourished one hundred and fifty years ago, now under Soviet control, but also, further to the west, Eisenach, where Martin Luther went to school and in whose castle, the Wartburg, he translated the Bible into German in 1521–2. The very heart of Germany, particularly of Protestant Germany, is nowadays in Russian hands, and eastern Europe has been swallowed within the Russian orbit.

Russian power extended beyond Germany through the Communist parties of western Europe. Soviet influence was extremely small in those countries where democratic labor ruled—Great Britain and the Scandinavian countries and also Germany, which was most immediately threatened by any Russian move; but it was strong in France and Italy, and free institutions were clearly in jeopardy in western Europe until the economy of these countries could be restored and stabilized. Clearly American aid was necessary.

Originally the United States gave support to the struggling national economies of the western and southern European countries through army funds, but when Britain had to withdraw her support from Greece in 1947, she developed a more systematic approach bolstering western Europe's resistance to the forces of Communist aggression. The Truman Doctrine, pledging American assistance to any country resisting Communist attacks, was proclaimed, and funds were provided to reinforce the Greek economy and military strength. But this move was only the beginning of a greater American effort to stabilize western Europe's economic and social foundations through the Marshall Plan. The European Recovery Administration, as the American legislation was officially called, went into effect in 1948.* It represented the renewed recognition of America's vital interest in western Europe, which had not declined as a result of the defeat of Hitler.

Indeed, with Russia's newly revealed power and expansion into eastern Europe and China, the stake of the United States in western Europe has grown greatly. The rump-Europe not at present under Soviet control comprises two hundred and seventy million people; it produces the most goods and enjoys the highest standard of living of any area outside of the United States. Its annual output is almost twice that of the U. S. S. R. and more than half of the production of the United States. There is no reason to doubt that western Europe's gross output could under certain circumstances approximate in the future that of the United States. Moreover, in spite of the vastly greater destruction of World War II, Europe recovered considerably faster after World War II than after World War I. In 1947, prior to the employment of Marshall funds, European production, excluding western Germany, already exceeded that of 1938. Putting European production in 1938 at 100, the figures were: 103 for 1947, 116 for 1948, 125 for 1949; or, with western Germany included: 86, 100, 114.† A note of caution should be added. The mere restoration of the 1938 production of Europe cannot save Europe, for her population has grown and she has lost most of her foreign assets. In addition, the production growth in the Soviet Union has been even greater in recent years. The comparative figures for the U. S. S. R. in 1947–9 were 93, 118, 141.‡

* H. S. Ellis: *The Economics of Freedom, The Progress and Future of Aid to Europe* (New York: 1950). Every student of present European affairs will find this book, recently issued under the auspices of the Council on Foreign Relations, indispensable.

† United Nations: *Economic Bulletin for Europe* (Geneva: 1950), Vol. II, p. 66.

‡ 1940 = 100.

If western Europe were to fall under Russian domination, the industrial and military power of the Soviet Union
would be increased alarmingly. It is the major national
interest of the United States to stave off this danger and
the greatest single task, if United States foreign policy is
to contain Russian expansion anywhere. A break of the
western European dike would in all probability mean the
loss of Africa as well, and thereby give the Soviet Union
tremendous advantages in a struggle for world domination.

The United States needs the continued existence of a free
Europe. If Europe were to turn Communist, the United
States would have to transform herself into a fully militar-
ized state, ready to meet an attack upon the Western
hemisphere. Not even in war would the initiative rest in
American hands. Moreover, the loss of a free Europe
would deprive the United States of many spiritual and intellectual resources that have contributed greatly to American life. American civilization has been a forceful expression of a new Western nation. In all fields of moral and
cultural endeavor the civilization of the United States has
proved its enormous creative capacity. The superior attitude
of most European intellectuals only shows their ignorance
of American life. But America has always drawn heavily
on the basic thought of Europe and received from the Old
World many invigorating ideas. Even in science this was
true as late as World War II. The development of
the atomic bomb rested to a large extent on the theoretical
research of European scholars. The United States would
lose not only political power but also intellectual and
moral strength if Europe were to come under Soviet domination.

On the other hand, the future of the European states
depends on the willingness of the United States to help in
their defense. The European political system has been replaced by an Atlantic system, and the North Atlantic Pact
of April, 1949, under which the United States, Canada, and
ten European nations pledged themselves to mutual support

in the case of an armed attack, simply expresses the new political reality. It remains to be seen to what extent the Soviet threat to western Europe will induce the European nations to unify their policies more closely. Unity is needed for defense and also for the rebuilding and expansion of the European economy. But there is no need for the complete merger of all the European states. Britain, even nowadays, fulfills a great function in the maintenance of world order outside of Europe, and she could not be fitted into a European union. The future progress of European unification hinges chiefly on the evolution of Franco-German relations. Europe, if she wants to live, will have to accept common arrangements for defense and internal prosperity, but she does not have to surrender her other diversified institutions and manners, which constitute her historical heritage, still precious in an age of mass civilization.

Bibliographical Note

THIS bibliographical note cannot aim at an exhaustive enumeration of studies relevant to the subjects treated in the narrative. The book is a determined attempt to condense the events of the international political history of modern Europe to the essentials. The bibliography intends to give the general reader some guidance only with regard to the most important books in the field. Primary sources have been excluded in the earlier period because they have been used in most cases by one or more generations of historians and can easily be found in their works. But in the period from 1918 to the present some of the most important primary sources have been named, since they have not yet been exploited by professional historical research. Works in foreign languages are not cited either, unless they are superior to comparable studies in the English language or are indispensable for the basic appraisal of the historical events under discussion. The arrangement of the bibliography is, of course, open to criticism on logical grounds. But it is hoped that the reader and even the professional student will find practical value in it.

GENERAL BIBLIOGRAPHY

A general bibliography, wisely selected and annotated, is G. M. Dutcher and others (eds.): *A Guide to Historical Literature* (New York: 1931). Naturally, after twenty years the *Guide* has become inadequate in many respects, particularly with regard to the history of the last fifty years. A good general bibliography is contained in R. R. Palmer: *A History of the Modern World* (New York: 1950) and for the period after 1900 in C. E. Black and E. C. Helmreich· *Twentieth Century Europe* (New York: 1950). An elaborate bibliography on the diplomatic history of nineteenth century Europe can be found in R. W. Seton-Watson: *Britain and Europe* (Cambridge: 1937). For the post-World-War-I period the two *Foreign Affairs* bibliographies are very serviceable: W. L. Langer and H. F. Armstrong: *Foreign Affairs Bibliography: 1919–32* (New York: 1933) and R. Woolbert: *Foreign Affairs Bibliography: 1932–42* (New York: 1945). For keeping abreast of recent publications the current issues of the

American Historical Review, the *Journal of Modern History, Foreign Affairs, International Affairs,* and other scholarly periodicals will have to be consulted.

GENERAL WORKS

FOR the general history of Europe since the eighteenth century the series *The Rise of Modern Europe,* edited by W. L. Langer (New York: 1934 ff.) will be found particularly useful. The series is not yet complete, but the following volumes have appeared: W. L. Dorn: *Competition for Empire, 1740–1763* (1940); L. Gershoy: *From Despotism to Revolution, 1763–1789* (1944); C. Brinton: *A Decade of Revolution, 1789–1799* (1934); G. Bruun: *Europe and the French Imperium, 1799–1814* (1938); F. B. Artz: *Reaction and Revolution, 1814–1832* (1934); R. C. Binkley: *Realism and Nationalism, 1852–1871* (1935); C. J. H. Hayes: *A Generation of Materialism, 1871–1900* (1941). The French series *Peuples et civilisations,* edited by L. Halphen and P. Sagnac (Paris: 1926 ff.) is valuable and comprises in its last two volumes relatively the best general history of the twentieth century written so far. G. Lefebvre: *La révolution française* (1930); *Napoléon* (1935); G. Weill: *L'éveil des nationalités et le mouvement libéral: 1815–1848* (1930); C. Pouthas: *Démocratie et capitalisme: 1848–1860* (1941); H. Hauser: *Du libéralisme à l'impérialisme: 1860–1878* (1939); M. Baumont: *L'essor industriel: 1878–1904* (1937), P. Renouvin: *La crise européenne et la grande guerre, 1914–1918* (1934); M. Baumont: *La faillite de la paix, 1918–1939* (1946; 2nd ed., 2 vols., 1951).

There is only one modern book covering the whole modern diplomatic history of Europe: W. Windelband: *Die auswärtige Politik der Grossmächte in der Neuzeit von 1494 bis zur Gegenwart* (3rd ed., Essen: 1936). Among English books the following deserve mention: R. B. Mowat: *A History of European Diplomacy, 1451–1789* (London: 1928); Sir Charles Petrie: *Diplomatic History, 1713–1933* (London: 1946). The Soviet view of diplomatic history is represented in V. P. Potemkin (ed.): *Histoire de la diplomatie,* 3 vols. (Paris:1946–7). (Cf. the critical review by A. Vagts in *World Politics* (1949) Vol. II, pp. 96–119). Diplomatic histories of individual nations of merit are A. W. Ward and G. P. Gooch (eds.): *The Cambridge History of British Foreign Policy, 1783–1919,* 3 vols. (Cambridge: 1922–3); R. W. Seton-Watson: *Britain in Europe, 1789–1914* (Cambridge: 1937); G. Vernadsky: *Political and Diplomatic History of Russia* (Boston: 1936); S. F. Bemis: *A Diplomatic History of the United States* (3rd ed., New York: 1950); T. A. Bailey: *A Diplomatic History of the American People* (4th ed., New York: 1950).

On the economic history of Europe a number of good general texts is available: H. Heaton: *Economic History of Europe* (rev. ed., New York: 1948); W. Bowden, M. Karpovich, and A. P. Usher: *An Economic History of Europe since 1750* (New York: 1937); S. B. Clough and C. W. Cole: *Economic History of Europe* (2nd ed., Boston: 1946). Of a more analytical nature are the important works of W. Sombart: *Der moderne Kapitalismus*, Vols. I and II (5th ed., Munich: 1922); Vol. III (Munich: 1928). Many of Sombart's ideas have been embodied in F. L. Nussbaum: *History of the Economic Institutions of Modern Europe* (New York: 1933). For the industrial revolution itself the study by P. Mantoux, first published in 1906, *The Industrial Revolution* (rev. ed., New York: 1935) is still indispensable. The slim volume by T. S. Ashton: *The Industrial Revolution, 1760–1830* (London: 1948) summarizes well the results of recent scholarship. No student of modern capitalism should miss the magnificent works of Sir John Clapham: *An Economic History of Modern Britain*, 3 vols. (Cambridge: 1926–38); *The Bank of England*, 2 vols. (Cambridge: 1944); *The Economic Development of France and Germany, 1815–1914* (4th ed., Cambridge: 1936). For the study of population problems see: A. Carr-Saunders: *World Population: Past Growth and Present Trends* (Oxford: 1936); D. Kirk: *Europe's Population in the Inter-War Years* (Geneva: 1946); F. W. Notestein *et al.*: *The Future Population of Europe and the Soviet Union* (Geneva: 1944).

The problem of nationalism in the nineteenth and twentieth centuries is best treated in *Nationalism, A Report by a Study Group of Members of the Royal Institute of International Affairs* (London: 1939). Another valuable, if more specialized, study is A. Cobban: *National Self-Determination* (London: 1944). C. J. H. Hayes: *The Historical Evolution of Modern Nationalism* (New York: 1931) and *Essays on Nationalism* (New York: 1926) are notable contributions to the subject. H. Kohn in his *The Idea of Nationalism* (New York: 1944) has treated the origins and background of modern nationalism up to the French Revolution. Over the last years H. Kohn has helped to elucidate the influence of national thinking in nineteenth century history by numerous articles.

The literature of European imperialism has found a bibliographer in L. J. Ragatz: *The Literature of European Imperialism, 1815–1939* (Washington, D.C.: 1944). Though the term is older, the book of the radical liberal English economist J. A. Hobson: *Imperialism* (1st ed., London: 1902; 3rd ed. 1938) exercised great influence on its usage in liberal, socialist, and communist thought. V. I. Lenin's *Imperialism, the Highest Stage of Capitalism*, written in 1916, had a world-shaking effect. The debate on imperialism is fully discussed by W. L. Langer: *The Diplomacy of Imperialism, 1890–1902*, 2 vols. (New York: 1935). Apart from the older book by P. T. Moon:

Imperialism and World Politics (New York: 1926) the following studies should be consulted: E. Staley: *War and the Private Investor* (Garden City, N. Y.: 1935) and L. C. Robbins: *The Economic Causes of War* (London: 1939).

For military affairs E. M. Earle (ed.): *Makers of Modern Strategy* (Princeton, N. J.: 1943) can serve as a general guide. A. Vagts: *History of Militarism* (New York: 1937) is packed with information on the history of army organization and military folklore. On naval power see Sir Herbert Richmond: *Statesmen and Sea Power* (2nd ed., Oxford: 1947); B. Brodie: *Seapower in the Machine Age* (2nd ed., Princeton, N. J.: 1943) and the brilliant article by H. Rosinski: "The Role of Sea Power in Global Warfare of the Future," *Brassey's Naval Annual* (1946), pp. 102–16.

CHAPTER I

AN interesting and stimulating discussion of the confines of Europe is contained in a recent book by the eminent Polish historian O. Halecki: *The Limits and Divisions of European History* (New York: 1950). Cf. also J. Bowle: *The Unity of European History* (London: 1948); C. Dawson: *The Making of Europe* (New York: 1945); E. Fischer: *The Passing of the European Age* (Cambridge, Mass.: 1943).

CHAPTER II

THE classic treatment of the European balance of power is L. Ranke's essay of 1833 *"Die grossen Mächte"*, which has become available in an American translation in T. H. Von Laue: *Leopold Ranke: The Formative Years* (Princeton, N. J.: 1950) pp. 181–218. The essay expressed Ranke's faith in the indestructible character of the European political system, which was built on the diversity of European nations. In his opinion this belief had been fully vindicated by the outcome of the Napoleonic wars and the Vienna settlement. He took the view that the national interests of the great powers were supreme over the internal and ideological struggles within states. This conception had a strong influence on the separation of diplomatic from general history (and not just in Germany) from which historical scholarship has not yet fully freed itself. An interesting example of the political consequences of Ranke's view of history is given by L. Dehio: "*Ranke und der deutsche Imperialismus*," *Historische Zeitschrift* (1950), Vol. 170, pp. 307–28. The same author has written a provocative study on the international history of modern Europe *Gleichgewicht oder Hegemonie* (Krefeld: 1948). For the eighteenth century diplomacy W. L. Dorn's book in the Langer series, mentioned above, is particularly good. The monographic study by D. Gerhard: *England und der Aufstieg Russlands* (Munich: 1933) should be mentioned not only on account of its significant subject but also because of its exemplary historical method, which succeeds in a synthesis of the political, economic, and social elements of history. Nobody should ever miss the picture that A. Sorel drew of eighteenth century diplomacy in his great *L'Europe et la révolution française*, 8 vols. (Paris: 1885–1904), of which the first part was translated by F. H. Herrick (Los Angeles, Calif.: 1947).

For the history of the Vienna settlement the various studies by C. K. Webster are particularly important: *The Congress of Vienna* (3rd ed., London: 1937); *The Foreign Policy of Castlereagh, 1812–1815* (London: 1931); *The Foreign Policy of Castlereagh, 1815–1822* (London: 1925). E. L. Woodward's collection *Three Studies in European Conservatism* contains a good brief study of Metternich (London: 1929), which was able to use the modern standard biography by H. von Srbik: *Metternich*, 2 vols. (Munich: 1925). C. Brinton: *The Lives of Talleyrand* (New York: 1936); cf. also A. D. Cooper: *Talleyrand* (New York: 1932). H. Nicolson: *The Congress of Vienna* (New York: 1946), in spite of its literary qualities, is less of an original contribution than most of the other works of the eminent student of diplomacy.

C. K. Webster's studies on Castlereagh are continued with H. W. V. Temperley's *The Foreign Policy of Canning* (London: 1925). For the American side of the history of these years cf. D. Perkins: *Hands Off: A History of the Monroe Doctrine* (Boston: 1941). For the Concert of Europe: W. A. Phillips: *The Confederation of Europe* (London: 1914); H. G. Schenk: *The Aftermath of the Napoleonic Wars: The Concert of Europe—An Experiment* (New York: 1947). On international change see E. L. Woodward's essay in his *War and Peace in Europe* (London: 1931); C. R. M. F. Cruttwell: *A History of Peaceful Change in the Modern World* (London: 1937).

Moving closer towards the middle of the century H. C. F. Bell: *Lord Palmerston*, 2 vols. (New York: 1936) deserves attention; also F. A. Simpson: *The Rise of Louis Napoleon* (2nd ed., Cambridge: 1925) and *Louis Napoleon and the Recovery of France, 1848–1856* (2nd ed., Cambridge: 1930); H. A. L. Fisher: *Bonapartism* (2nd ed., London: 1914); A. Guérard: *Napoleon III* (Cambridge, Mass.:

1943); A. Pingaud: *"La Politique extérieure du Second Empire," Revue Historique* (1927), Vol. CLVI pp. 46–68; H. Temperley: *England and the Near East: The Crimea* (Cambridge: 1936); W. R. Thayer: *Life and Times of Cavour* (Boston: 1911).

CHAPTER III

ALTHOUGH the Bismarck literature is staggering and contains many fine monographs, no adequate biography or, at least, general appraisal of his statesmanship exists. The biography by C. G. Robertson: *Bismarck* (London: 1919) is still the leading English book in spite of the fact that only in the subsequent twenty years have the fundamental sources been published from German archives. See the article by G. P. Gooch: "The Study of Bismarck" in his *Studies in German History* (London: 1948). The continuous flow of new material produced an avalanche of specialized studies but no satisfactory general treatment, partly, no doubt, a result of the political situation in Germany. The last German biography of Bismarck was written by A. O. Meyer during World War II (Stuttgart: 1948), but Meyer's scholarship was marred by his absolute admiration of the chancellor. On the other side E. Eyck's big biography, 3 vols. (Zurich: 1941–4) is an oversimplified appraisal by a German democrat. An abstract of this biography is available in English: *Bismarck and the German Empire* (London: 1950). Cf. also F. Darmstaedter: *Bismarck and the Creation of the Second Reich* (London: 1949).

For the economic aspects of German unification we have the thorough study by W. O. Henderson: *The Zollverein* (Cambridge: 1939). H. Friedjung: *The Struggle for Supremacy in Germany, 1859–1866* (London: 1935), a condensed translation of a work by an Austrian historian, first published in 1897, is still useful, though it should be compared with C. W. Clark: *Franz Joseph and Bismarck: The Diplomacy of Austria Before the War of 1866* (Cambridge, Mass.: 1934).

A. J. P. Taylor: *The Habsburg Monarchy* (rev. ed., London: 1948) is a good book on the Austro-Hungarian problem. J. Redlich: *Emperor Francis Joseph of Austria* (New York: 1929) presents a biographical approach.

The very extensive research done after World War I in the European diplomacy of the period between 1871–90 has been digested and well appraised in the solid work of W. L. Langer: *European Alliances and Alignments* (New York: 1931; 2nd ed., 1950). The same author has given us the best treatment of the period from 1890–1902 in his *Diplomacy of Imperialism* (New York: 1935). Going beyond the diplomatic field R. J. Sontag has treated Anglo-German relations in the second half of the century in his *Germany and England: Background of Conflict, 1848–94* (New York: 1938). B. H. Sumner's book *Russia and the Balkans, 1870–1880* (Oxford: 1937) ably presents another important special problem of the period.

On the colonial policies of the powers reference is made to the following works: P. Knaplund: *The British Empire, 1815–1939* (New York: 1941); S. H. Roberts: *History of French Colonial Policy, 1870–1925*, 2 vols. (London: 1929); M. E. Townsend: *The Rise and Fall of Germany's Colonial Empire, 1884–1918* (New York: 1930); H. R. Rudin: *The Germans in the Cameroons, 1884–1914* (New Haven, Conn.: 1938); C. Hollis: *Italy in Africa* (London: 1941). On the Far East see: J. W. Pratt: *Expansionists of 1898: The Acquisitions of Hawaii and the Spanish Islands* (Baltimore: 1936); and *America's Colonial Experiment* (New York: 1950); A. W. Griswold: *The Far-Eastern Policy of the United States* (New York: 1938); Sir John Pratt: *The Expansion of Europe into the Far East* (London: 1947); A. Lobanov-Rostovsky: *Russia and Asia* (New York: 1933); B. H. Sumner: *Tsardom and Imperialism in the Far East and the Middle East, 1880–1914* (London: 1942); R. Kerner: *The Urge for the Sea, the Course of Russian History* (Berkeley, Calif.: 1942).

Economic problems of the period are treated by P. W. L. Ashley: *Modern Tariff History: Germany, United States, France* (3rd ed., New York: 1920); H. Levy: *The New Industrial System* (London: 1936); W. F. Bruck: *Social and Economic History of Germany, 1888–1938* (Oxford: 1938); A. Gerschenkron: *Bread and Democracy in Germany* (New York: 1943).

CHAPTER IV

A good summary of diplomatic history of a period larger than the one treated in this chapter is R. J. Sontag: *European Diplomatic History, 1871–1932* (New York: 1933); cf. also E. M. Carroll: *Germany and the Great Powers, 1866–1914* (New York: 1938).

Among works on the diplomatic events that led to World War I stand out: S. B. Fay: *The Origins of the World War*, 2 vols. (New York: 1928; 2nd ed. 1930); B. E. Schmitt: *The Coming of the War*, 2 vols. (New York: 1930); for the last phase also P. Renouvin: *The Immediate Origins of the War* (New Haven, Conn.: 1928). A biographical method was chosen by G. P. Gooch: *Before the War—Studies in Diplomacy*, 2 vols. (London: 1936–38).

The military history of World War I is the subject of an English and an American book: C. R. Cruttwell: *A History of the Great War, 1914–1918* (Oxford: 1934) and J. F. McEntee: *Military His-*

tory of the World War (New York: 1937). Both the military and political events of the War were depicted by W. S. Churchill: *The World Crisis, 1911–1918* (London: 1923–9), a truly great book, which is perhaps not in every respect critical history but which brings the reader closer to the actual atmosphere than any academic work.

On Russia during the War see Sir Bernard Pares: *The Fall of the Russian Monarchy* (New York: 1939); B. E. Nolde: *Russia in the Economic War* (Oxford: 1928); I. N. Danilov: *La Russie dans la guerre mondiale, 1914–1917* (Paris: 1927); J. W. Wheeler-Bennett: *The Forgotten Peace: Brest Litovsk* (New York: 1939).

For Britain and France see the remarkable book by D. W. Brogan: *The Development of Modern France* (New York: 1940). Also A. Pingaud: *Histoire diplomatique de la France pendant la grande guerre,* 2 vols. (Paris: 1938); F. W. Hirst: *Consequences of the War to Great Britain* (Oxford: 1934).

For the Central Powers: J. Redlich: *Austrian War Government* (Vienna: 1929); E. Glaise-Horstenau: *The Collapse of the Austro-Hungarian Empire* (New York: 1930); O. Jaszi: *The Dissolution of the Habsburg Monarchy* (Chicago: 1929). An excellent analytical history of German politics during World War I is A. Rosenberg: *The Birth of the German Republic* (New York: 1931); an exceptionally fine book dealing with German history during World War I and thereafter is J. W. Wheeler-Bennett: *Hindenburg, the Wooden Titan* (New York: 1936). H. R. Rudin presents a good study of the German collapse in his *Armistice 1918* (New Haven, Conn.: 1944), while Sir Frederick Maurice: *The Armistices of 1918* (London: 1943) deals with all the armistices.

The extensive literature dealing with the entrance of the United States in the War is listed in Bemis's and Bailey's American diplomatic histories.

We have no critical history of the Paris Peace Conference, partly because up to World War II only private sources were available, partly because we need a historical reappraisal in the light of World War II. The publication by the United States Department of State of thirteen massive volumes from 1942–7 has created a great opportunity for research on the peace conference, of which little use has been made so far. (*Papers Relating to the Foreign Relations of the United States: The Paris Peace Conference, 1919*). H. W. V. Temperley (ed.): *A History of the Peace Conference,* 6 vols. (London: 1920–4), written by British and American experts at Paris, is not so much a history of the Conference as a discussion of the subjects with which the Conference had to deal. H. Nicolson's *Peacemaking 1919* (London: 1934) is an absorbing introduction to the atmosphere of Paris. Cf. also G. B. Noble: *Policies and Opinions at Paris, 1919* (New York: 1935). P. Birdsall: *Versailles, Twenty Years After* (New York: 1941) still remains a valuable monograph.

CHAPTER V

THE best introduction to the historical situation created by the Peace Conference of Paris is A. J. Toynbee: *The World after the Peace Conference* (London: 1926). This small but rich volume was the prologue to Toynbee's *Survey of International Affairs,* published since 1924 in annual volumes under the auspices of the Royal Institute of International Affairs (Chatham House), to which every student of the interwar period must feel deeply indebted.

The literature of the League of Nations is very large. Only three works will be mentioned here, of which the first is the one that best places the League of Nations in a historical perspective, while the last succeeds most in demonstrating the practical operations of the League: A. Zimmern: *The League of Nations and the Rule of Law* (New York: 1936); C. K. Webster: *The League of Nations in Theory and Practice* (London: 1933); F. Morley: *The Society of Nations* (Washington, D.C.: 1932).

The impact of World War I on Europe is dealt with in the following books: A. Mendelssohn Bartholdy: *The War and German Society* (New Haven, Conn.: 1936); D. Mitrany: *The Effect of the War in Southeastern Europe* (New Haven, Conn.: 1936).

For the interwar period in Britain cf. A. J. Toynbee: *The Conduct of British Empire Foreign Relations since the Peace Settlement* (London: 1928); E. A. Walker: *The British Empire: Its Structure and Spirit* (London: 1943). The actual policy of the British dominions is well expounded in the careful study by G. M. Carter: *The British Commonwealth and International Security* (Toronto: 1947). On Brittain herself see R. Graves and A. Hodge: *The Long Weekend: A Social History of Great Britain, 1918–1939* (London: 1940); A. C. Pigou: *Aspects of British Economic History, 1918–1925* (London: 1947); A. Siegfried: *England's Crisis* (New York: 1931); H. Nicolson: *Curzon: The Last Phase, 1919–1925* (New York: 1934); W. N. Medlicott: *British Foreign Policy Since Versailles* (London: 1940).

For France, apart from D. W. Brogan, cf. G. Peel: *The Economic Policy of France* (London: 1937); S. B. Clough: *France: A History of National Economics* (New York: 1939). On French foreign policy: W. d'Ormesson: *France* (London: 1939).

Italy in this period can be studied through the following books: A. Rossi: *The Rise of Italian Fascism, 1918–1922* (London: 1938); H. W. Schneider: *Making the Fascist State* (New York: 1928); H. Finer: *Mussolini's Italy* (London: 1935); R. Albrecht Carrié: *Italy at the Peace Conference* (New York: 1938); M. I. Currey: *Italian Foreign Policy, 1918–1932* (London: 1932); M. H. H. Macartney and P.

Cremona: *Italian Foreign and Colonial Policy, 1914–1937* (London: 1938), the best available account. A study of wider scope is E. Monroe: *The Mediterranean in Politics* (London: 1938).

For the Eastern European nations see L. Pasvolsky: *Economic Nationalism in the Danubian States* (New York: 1928); J. O. Crane: *The Little Entente* (New York: 1931); R. Machray: *The Struggle for the Danube and the Little Entente, 1929–1938* (London: 1938); R. J. Kerner: *The Balkan Conferences and the Balkan Entente, 1930–1935* (Berkeley, Calif.: 1936); F. J. Vondracek: *The Foreign Policy of Czechoslovakia, 1918–1935* (New York: 1937); J. F. Morrow: *The Peace Settlement in the German-Polish Borderlands* (London: 1936). Cf. also the three reports issued by the Royal Institute of International Affairs: *The Balkan States: I. Economic: A Review of the Economic and Financial Development of Albania, Bulgaria, Greece, Roumania, and Yugoslavia since 1919* (London: 1936); *The Baltic States* (London: 1938); *South-Eastern Europe: A Political and Economic Survey* (London: 1939). In addition see C. A. Macartney: *Hungary and Her Successors: The Treaty of Trianon and Its Consequences, 1919–1937* (London: 1937) and the same author's *The Social Revolution in Austria* (London: 1926). The best work on southeastern Europe is H. Seton-Watson: *Eastern Europe Between the Wars, 1918–1941* (2nd ed., Cambridge: 1946).

For Weimar Germany, in addition to Wheeler-Bennett's *Hindenburg* see: J. W. Angell: *The Recovery of Germany* (rev. ed., New Haven: 1932); H. Kessler: *Walter Rathenau* (London: 1929); R. T. Clark: *The Fall of the German Republic* (London: 1935); S. W. Halperin: *Germany Tried Democracy* (New York: 1946).

On the whole the most satisfactory brief survey of the diplomatic events of the interwar period is G. M. Gathorne-Hardy: *A Short History of International Affairs, 1920–1939* (4th ed., London: 1950). Cf. also E. H. Carr: *International Relations Since the Peace Treaties* (rev. ed., London: 1941) and the more interpretative study by the same author: *The Twenty Years' Crisis* (London: 1940). The best historical monographic study of a key problem of European political history in the interwar period is W. M. Jordan: *Great Britain, France and the German Problem, 1918–1939* (London: 1943). Another good monograph is A. Wolfers: *Britain and France Between Two Wars* (New York: 1940).

In addition to J. M. Keynes's books on reparations cf. K. Bergmann: *The History of Reparations* (New York: 1927); Sir Andrew McFadyean: *Reparations Reviewed* (London: 1930); H. G. Moulton and L. Pasvolsky: *War Debts and World Prosperity* (Washington, D.C.: 1932); J. W. Wheeler-Bennett: *The Wreck of Reparations, being the Political Background of the Lausanne Agreement, 1932* (New York: 1933). On the disarmament problem see J. W. Wheeler-Bennett: *The Pipe Dream of Peace* (London: 1934).

CHAPTER VI

THE world economic crisis of 1929 and after is treated in H. V. Hodson: *Slump and Recovery, 1929–1937* (London: 1938); L. C. Robbins: *The Great Depression* (London: 1934). Cf. also G. Haberler: *Prosperity and Depression* (Geneva: 1937) and W. A. Brown: *The International Gold Standard Re-interpreted* (New York: 1940); League of Nations: *The Course and Control of Inflation: A Review of Monetary Experience in Europe after World War I* (Princeton, N. J.: 1946). A Soviet interpretation is E. Varga: *The Great Crisis and its Political Consequences* (New York: 1935).

For the rise of Nazism and the Nazi state the following books are recommended: K. Heiden: *A History of National Socialism* (New York: 1935) and *Der Führer: Hitler's Rise to Power* (Boston: 1944); C. B. Hoover: *Germany Enters the Third Reich* (New York: 1934). The altogether most informative and penetrating work on the Nazi state is F. L. Neumann: *Behemoth: the Structure and Practice of National Socialism* (new ed., New York: 1944). Cf. also K. Loewenstein: *Hitler's Germany* (New York: 1940); S. Neumann: *Permanent Revolution* (New York: 1942); W. Ebenstein: *The Nazi State* (New York: 1943); C. W. Guillebaud: *The Economic Recovery of Germany* (London: 1939); O. Nathan: *The Nazi Economic System: Germany's Mobilization for War* (Durham, N. C.: 1944).

British policy after 1933 is discussed by R. W. Seton-Watson: *Britain and the Dictators* (Cambridge: 1939) and *After Munich* (London: 1939); K. Feiling: *The Life of Neville Chamberlain* (London: 1947).

For France in the thirties see H. W. Ehrmann: *French Labor from Popular Front to Liberation* (New York: 1947); C. A. Micaud: *The French Right and Nazi Germany, 1933–1939* (Durham, N. C.: 1943).

Russian foreign policy is best treated by M. Beloff: *The Foreign Policy of Soviet Russia, 1929–1941*, 2 vols. (London: 1947–8). For the early period see L. Fisher: *The Soviets in World Affairs*, 2 vols. (New York: 1930). Cf. also D. J. Dallin: *Soviet Russia's Foreign Policy, 1939–1942* (New Haven, Conn.: 1943) and *Soviet Russia and the Far East* (New Haven, Conn.: 1948); T. A. Taracouzio: *War and Peace in Soviet Diplomacy* (Cambridge, Mass.: 1940); M. M. Laserson: *Russia and the Western World* (New York: 1945); I. Deutscher: *Stalin* (New York: 1949); F. Borkenau: *The Communist International* (London: 1938); M. Ebon: *World Communism Today* (New York: 1948).

The best studies on the European diplomacy during the thirties are J. W. Wheeler-Bennett: *Munich: Prologue to Tragedy* (London: 1948) and L. B. Namier: *Diplomatic Prelude, 1938–1939* (London:

1948). E. Wiskemann studied the background of the Munich crisis in her *Czechs and Germans* (New York: 1938) and Nazi-Fascist relations in *The Rome-Berlin Axis* (New York: 1949).

The international policy of the interwar period has still to be written and viewed with critical reserve, since the official secret documents are still in the process of publication. The most important single publication for the whole period is E. L. Woodward and R. Butler (eds.): *Documents on British Foreign Policy, 1919–1939,* (London: 1946 ff.). In the first series, starting 1919, thus far 3 vols., in the second, beginning 1929, 4 vols., in the third, intended to cover the years 1938–9, 3 vols. have appeared. The American publication *Papers Relating to the Foreign Relations of the United States,* published by the United States Department of State, now goes through 1933 and contains a great deal of material relevant to European diplomacy. The Nuremberg documents and the publication of the German Foreign Office documents are fully quoted in footnote p. 152 of this book. The official documentation is supplemented by a wealth of diaries, documents, and memoirs coming from private sources, chiefly in France, Germany, Britain, and Italy. L. B. Namier: *Europe in Decay, 1936–1940* (London: 1950) reviews a good many of them. For a full listing of those books published in English see the bibliography in R. R. Palmer: *A History of the Modern World* (New York: 1950).

For the military history see the chronology in R. W. Shugg and H. A. DeWeerd: *World War II: A Concise History* (Washington, D.C.: 1946). An interpretative history is J. F. C. Fuller: *The Second World War, 1939–1945* (London: 1948). The eastern front is treated in W. E. D. Allen and P. Muratoff: *The Russian Campaigns 1941–43* (New York: 1944); *The Russian Campaigns of 1944–45* (New York: 1946). General D. D. Eisenhower: *Crusade in Europe* (Garden City, N. Y.: 1948) deals also with some political problems. A grandiose treatment of the military and political events of World War II is given in W. S. Churchill's magnificent commentaries on the war, *The Second World War*, of which four volumes have appeared covering to the spring of 1943—*The Gathering Storm,* Vol. I; *Their Finest Hour,* Vol. II; *The Grand Alliance,* Vol. III; *The Hinge of Fate,* Vol. IV (Boston: 1948–50).

Among the sources for the study of American participation in World War II the following are most important: C. Hull: *Memoirs* (New York: 1948); R. E. Sherwood: *Roosevelt and Hopkins* (New York: 1948); H. L. Stimson and McG. Bundy: *On Active Service in War and Peace* (New York: 1948). Cf. also E. R. Stettinius, Jr.: *Lend-Lease: Weapon for Victory* (New York: 1944) and *Roosevelt and the Russians: The Yalta Conference* (Garden City, N. Y.: 1949); J. F. Byrnes: *Speaking Frankly* (New York: 1947); J. R. Deane: *The Strange Alliance* (New York: 1947).

A brief historical review of United States foreign policy after 1933 is A. Nevins: *The New Deal and World Affairs* (New Haven, Conn.: 1950). W. L. Langer: *Our Vichy Gamble* (New York: 1947) gives a fully documented if overly apologetic, history of American wartime policy towards Vichy. On American military government planning and operations see H. Holborn: *American Military Government: Its Organization and Policies* (Washington, D.C.: 1947); W. L. Friedman: *The Allied Military Government of Germany* (London: 1947); C. J. Friedrich *et al.: American Experiences in Military Government in World War II* (New York: 1948); G. A. Almond *et al.: The Struggle for Democracy in Germany* (Chapel Hill, N. C.: 1949).

On France during World War II cf. D. M. Pickle: *France between the Republics* (London: 1946). For the anti-Hitler movement in Germany see F. Ford: "The Twentieth of July in the History of the German Resistance," *American Historical Review* (1946), Vol. LI, pp. 609–26. A. W. Dulles: *The German Underground* (New York: 1947); H. Rothfels: *The German Opposition to Hitler* (Hillsdale, Ill.: 1948).

CHAPTER VII

THE best work on the United Nations is L. M. Goodrich and E. Hambro: *Charter of the United Nations: Commentary and Documents* (rev. ed., Boston: 1949).

On the economic recovery and rehabilitation of Europe compare the *Economic Survey of Europe in 1947, 1948, 1949*, prepared by the United Nations Economic Commission for Europe (Geneva: 1948–50). See also S. E. Harris: *The European Recovery Program* (Cambridge, Mass.: 1948) and the fine volume edited under the auspices of the Council on Foreign Relations, H. E. Ellis: *The Economics of Freedom: The Progress and Future of Aid to Europe* (New York: 1950).

The origins of the Fourth Republic have been ably described by G. Wright: *The Reshaping of French Democracy* (New York: 1948). On Italy, see M. Grindrod: *The New Italy* (London: 1947); on Germany, L. D. Clay: *Decision in Germany* (Garden City, N. Y.: 1950); F. L. Neumann: "German Democracy 1950," *International Conciliation* (May, 1950), no. 461; on southeastern Europe H. Seton-Watson: *Eastern Europe, 1941–46* (Cambridge: 1950).

See finally W. Lippmann: *The Cold War: A Study in U. S. Foreign Policy* (New York: 1947); E. M. Earle: "A Half-Century of American Foreign Policy: Our Stake in Europe, 1898–1948," *Political Science Quarterly* (1949), Vol. LXIV, pp. 168–88.

Index

Index